Strands of Memory
~ *Epilogue*

Sweet and Bittersweet Memories and Meditations

William R. Tracey, Ed.D.

Heartfelt thanks go to
Maura Tarbania, my daughter,
and
Stephen Mottley, my friend,
for their help and iPad/computer expertise
to produce
the color cover and author's photo
for this volume of
Strands of Memory— Epilogue

Order this book online at www.trafford.com
or email orders@trafford.com

Most Trafford titles are also available at major online book retailers.

Printed in the United States of America.

ISBN: 978-1-4907-4499-5 (sc)
ISBN: 978-1-4907-4498-8 (e)

Trafford rev. 09/08/2014

 www.trafford.com

North America & international
toll-free: 1 888 232 4444 (USA & Canada)
fax: 812 355 4082

Dedication

For My Wife
Kathleen Lucille (Doheny) Tracey

For My Children
William Raymond Tracey, Jr.
Kevin Thomas Tracey
Brian John Tracey
Kathleen Lucille Bastille
Maura Gail Tarbania
Sean Michael Tracey

For My Grandchildren
Tamra Lee Letellier Lumpkin
Jacqueline Marie Munson
Michele Marie Coffman
Sean Keenan Letellier
Laine Tracey Tarbania
William Raymond Tracey III
Timothy Patrick Tracey
Kathleen Elizabeth Tracey
Victor Carrillo Tracey
Kolby Lynne Tracey
Kaylyn Michelle Tracey
Siara Carrillo Tracey

For My Great Grandchildren
Kaila Lee Lumpkin
Grace Marie Munson
David Matthew Munson

For My Friend and Companion
Else-Marie Birgit Bowe

Be calm and serene
Change your attitude toward life
By will and prayer

Contents

Grace is a first-rate
Relationship with your God
Cultivate that bond

Foreword

his book concludes the saga of the Tracey-O'Neill—the oose ends" of the earlier volumes of Strands, the life and mes of an Irish-French Canadian (with a smattering of merican Indian, Spanish, and Swiss ancestors). When I ompleted the four earlier volumes — *Stands of Memory, rands of Memory Revisited, Strands of Memory Reprised,* and *rands of Memory My Swan Song,* I believed that I had xhausted the subject—that there was nothing left to write oout. I was very wrong. I have remembered so many subjects, emories, incidents, and mental meanderings in the two years nce the publication *of My Swan Song* that I now have the ontents of at least one additional book. Unfortunately, time id my advancing age will prevent the extension of this writing enre from continuing indefinitely. So this volume must be my st song, rather than just an encore or curtain call. Regretfully, have neither enough time nor the energy to undertake another olume.

herefore, this book is a collection of poems, mainly free verse at I have written over the last two years. My hope is that ome verses are insightful, but others are likely to be viewed as edantic or mundane. Realistically, some poems are reasonably ood verse and others may well be mediocre. Nevertheless, all them come from my heart. I make no excuses or apologies or that.

ome of the verses were written for Kathleen Lucille Tracey, y late spouse, lover. friend, and supporter for 56 wonderful ears. Others were written for my children, grandchildren, eat grandchildren, their spouses, other relatives, and my friends. More than a few verses were written for my lifeline my companion, and best friend for the last 14 years, Else Marie Bowe. Still others were simply reflections and ruminations about life and the events that befall mortals.

This series of anthologies is written primarily for my descendants — my children, grandchildren, great grandchildren, godchildren—and for my cousins, nieces nephews, and close friends. They are the people I love with all my heart and soul. My wife Kathleen made that point beautifully in a note she left in her own handwriting only a few months before she died. It read, "Love in your heart is not there to stay. Love is not love until you give it away!" She was so right!

All of the verses in this volume commemorate people who were very important in my life. Their love, friendship, support courage, and strengths have been an inspiration to me. This verse is my way of memorializing them and sharing them with each other and the world.

Fortunately for me, poetry as an art form now allows writers to record their life experiences and share their poetic vision with others in a great variety of styles and forms, from more or less intricate rhyme schemes to free verse, a complete lack of rhyme. Although none of the poems in this collection involve complex rhyming, they include both verse in simple rhyming and straightforward narrative forms.

I know that these verses reveal more about William Raymond (O'Neill) Tracey than most men would like to have exposed to the view of others, particularly to the members of their xtended family. But, I have always been a realist. I want my imily and friends to know the real person that I am —my reams, my fantasies, my weaknesses, my naiveté. So, there ·e very few things that remain hidden – and those are ithheld only because I believe that they would be hurtful to :hers if revealed.

utting my feelings and emotions into words and allowing my ·ved ones to experience with me the things that troubled, hurt, eased, or delighted me, helped me to heal and made my life ore meaningful and rewarding. Being able to express myself rough the written word and share my thoughts and feelings ith others are true blessings.

 summary, the verses that follow represent the distilled ssence of my long life — impressions and visions that I hope ill inspire readers at this point in their journey through life. I ope that they enjoy them.

 hope and pray that the people to whom this volume is ·dicated will remember me with forbearance and love – as ell as in their prayers. I also hope that they and those they ·ve will have good health, happiness, and all of the things that ill be useful to them in the plan of God.

'ith deepest respect and love to you all, from your Dad, ·ppi, Grand Poppi, Abuelo, Godfather, cousin, uncle, and iend, Bill.

William Raymond (O'Neill) Tracey

Take care of yourself
Enjoy healthful food and drink
Live a lengthy life

Love

There's a perfect match
For everyone in the world
Don't limit your search

About My Verse
Love Stories or Amorous Sonnets

These are the objects, types, dimensions,
and venues of free or rhyming heartfelt verse.
They are about or concerned with
people, communities, families, friends,
adults, teenagers, children,
eras, times, places, occasions, events,
circumstances, experiences, perspectives,
adversity, grief, sorrow, mourning,
remembrance, nature, life, and death.
They are typically significant, meaningful,
crucial, even momentous, happenings
that have important emotional impacts.
results, or consequences.
They are, in essence, spirit, or core,
the songs or requiems of my life.

My First Love

The is no uncertainty or doubt about it.
She was my very first true love.
Of course, I experienced puppy love
when I was much younger:
at age five, Kathleen, my next-door neighbor;
ages six and seven, Mary, at St. Mary's in Milford;
and ages ten to fourteen, Eleanor, at St. Leo's in Leominster.
And, naturally, I enjoyed the company of many lovely,
even beautiful, girls during my adolescent years.
They included girls with Irish, Polish, Italian, French Canadian
Native American, Spanish, Greek, and Yankee heritage.
Yes, I hugged and kissed all of them
with great feeling, affection, and enthusiasm,
but I remained a male virgin until I married.
*****

My very first true love arrived following my graduation
from Leominster High School in June 1940.
Our courtship continued until just before Christmas in 1941.
During that summer I was employed
at the Whitney Reed Company,
a hobbyhorse manufacturer in Leominster.
In January 1941, I moved to a job as a shortage chaser
at the Whitney Reed Company, maker of Arrow Shirts,
in Leominster.
I met Lucille at the Dolly McDaid School of Dancing on Nort
Street in Fitchburg, which I attended free of charge
because I helped Dolly teach ballroom dancing
to the girls in her classes.
*****

Lucille was the second girl (the first was Jean)
that attracted my attention and intense interest —
not just because she was a graceful, talented, and exceptional
dance partner but also because she was pretty, personable,
and a well-endowed young woman. She completely charmed,
captivated, and enchanted me with her well-modulated voice,
musical laughter, physical attributes,
and what soon became genuinely shared attraction.
To put it succinctly, I was hooked, and at that time,
believed that I was captured and enslaved for life.

*****

am convinced that genuine love first happens in the teen years,
whether early or late, but it invariably occurs in those years.
Although infatuation or beguilement to or by the opposite sex
may occur as early as age five or six,
credible love materializes in early, mid, or late adolescence
when the body matures, hormones take charge,
and the individual becomes conscious of
and attracted to people of the opposite (sometimes same) sex.
veryone can remember the emotions that dominated thoughts,
feelings, wants, needs, and desires, and during that period,
prevailed over everything, even the need
for peer or parental approval.
Often, later in life, things happen that cause the memories
of a love of long ago to kick in.
The source may be a place, a scent, a voice, a photo, even a
song, which awakens those reminiscences.

*****

So, why did we break up?
Its cause resided in me: insecurity and vulnerability,
traceable to the loss of my birth mother and my rearing
by a jealous, disparaging, and alcoholic foster father,
and, in direct contrast, a loving and supportive foster mother.

-5-

The direct cause: I learned that she had dated Jim once
late in our courtship that caused me feelings of distrust,
betrayal, and jealousy.
Although certain that one-time date was completely innocent
it was more than my youthful scruples
and self-righteous conscience
could deal with calmly and intelligently.
I was truly ready at that crucial time
to propose marriage.
I planned to purchase an engagement ring
but changed my mind
and instead bought her a friendship ring,
which I gave to her at Christmas.
That was our last date.
*****

During the Christmas season and Winter Carnival
at Fitchburg State in 1941, I met a classmate, Kathleen.
As president and leaders of the Class of 1944,
Kathleen and I were
often required to work together on party preparations,
entertainment, sleigh rides, dances, and other college events.
Then seriously on the rebound, I fell in love,
that time for good.
It had to be an intervention from Above.
Kathleen had made a commitment to enter the convent of the
Sisters of the Presentation of Mary
upon completing one year at FSTC.
That promise was made to her uncle, Father Bernard,
who needed to make certain that she wanted to become a nun.
We soon became engaged, despite the disapproval of her
family, particularly her aunts.
*****

ather Bernard at St. Bernard's Church married us July 1, 1944,
two days after I graduated from the US Naval Reserve
Midshipman's School at Columbia University in New York,
where I was commissioned an ensign
and assigned duty with the Pacific Fleet,
home-based in Honolulu, Hawaii.
*****

I never forgot Lucille and have thought about her countless
times in the last 60+ years, particularly during the 4 years
following Kathleen's death in October 1997 after 53 years of
marriage, six children, and twelve grandchildren.
She and I have seen each other only twice during those long
years — once at a dance at the Worcester Auditorium and
nother time at Kathleen and Eddie's high school class reunion.
On both occasions we danced together — where we reclaimed
ur earlier repute as accomplished and idyllic dancing partners.
*****

Unquestionably, she has made a lasting impression on my life.
can now say, without shame, guilt, or dishonor to Kathleen's
memory, that I truly loved her and that I still have
profound affection for her,
as well as true concern for her well-being
and tender feelings for and about her.
cherish our current long-distance contacts by phone and notes,
as well as our platonic relationship, as we share our
experiences, memories, and current interests, and activities.

Haiku

There's a perfect mate
For everyone in the world
Don't limit your search

For Else-Marie on Her 74th Birthday

This has been a very difficult year
for both of us, but especially for you.
I know how much you have suffered
daily with back, shoulder, hip, and leg pain.
Yet, you remained equal to the duties and tasks
required by Cumberland Farms.

And, despite your discomfort and agonizing pain,
you continued to wait on customers
with your unusual grace, courtesy, and efficiency.
You are, in truth, a remarkable woman,
one that I am exceptionally fortunate to know,
appreciate, value, and love.

In point of fact, I don't know what I would do
if you were unable to continue performing
the laundry, shopping, and housekeeping tasks
that you have been doing for me
for the past ten or more years.

However, you mean much more to me
than a friend and helpmate.
You are my loyal, faithful, trusted,
steadfast, reliable, captivating,
and, most important of all,
devoted and loving companion,

Truly you are my gift from God
during my last years on earth.
I wonder if you realize how important
you are every day in my life,

how I look forward eagerly to your arrival,
how I value our nightly and often daily
(although brief) phone conversations,
and how lonesome I am
when you are unable to come
and stay with me over night.

However, I do recognize and understand
that you have other things
that require, even demand, your attention —
visits of Clarence, Kiana, and friends,
doctors' appointments, house and property
maintenance and repair,
personal business, and other matters.

So, I ask your forgiveness and patience
with me when I am too demanding
of your presence and attention.
Always remember that I love you!
HAPPY BIRTHDAY!

Haiku

Remember this truth
Happiness lies in the heart
Not in the venue

The key to good health:
Stay positive in outlook
Don't sweat the small stuff

For Sean T. on His 54th Birthday

This free verse is written for someone very special.
On this auspicious and propitious day
fifty-four years ago
God blessed me by giving you to your Mom and me
as our sixth child and fourth loving son.
I pray every night that He will bless you
with everything that you need,
everything that is truly good,
for you and your wonderful and talented family.
And I also pray that His love
will always guide your way.
For the gifts with which you have been blessed
you are truly admired and loved!
For you and Lina are two of those rare people
who exemplify and keep the true spirit of family
glowing brightly and steadfastly
throughout the year.
For you are authentic reflections of God's love.
Remember that your mother and father
loved you and always will.
regardless of where they may be.
Let me close this missive
by repeating an old sailor's plea and prayer
for his youngest son and heir:
May you have blue skies and calm following seas
on your birthday and every day of the years to come.

HAPPY BIRTHDAY!

The Origins of Love — An Enigma

The sources of the attraction of two persons
to each other are almost infinite in both kind and
number. However, they invariably involve all of
the human senses: touch, sight, hearing, taste,
smell, and, most of all the brain —
and its connection to human emotions,
sensibilities, experiences, preferences, and
attitudes, all of which are unique to the individual.
That is why it is so often said that there is a nearly perfect
match for everyone in the world —
in terms of race, color, height, weight, appearance,
sex, or sexual orientation, intelligence, personality,
nd just about every other distinguishing trait or characteristic.
he challenge to every man and woman is to find that person at
the right time, place, and under the right circumstances.
It is often true that the match-up is neither
nderstood nor accepted by those close to the couple involved.
person is attracted to another in ways and for reasons that are
frequently incomprehensible to others.
How can anyone explain why beautiful women
often choose plain (even ugly) men as their mates
— or why handsome men choose unattractive
(even homely) women as their lovers?
And why do brilliant men often choose
obviously feather-brained women as their consorts
—and bright women choose unlettered or not so bright men as
heir lovers? So, Eros arrives in unpredictable ways, and that is
the underlying reason for unlikely yet long-lasting and very
successful unions.

For Lucille on Her 91st Birthday

Here are some of the clichés
That is apt and proper for my first true love, Lucille Dolores
Lucille is as:
Quick as a cat
Busy as a bee
Bright as a silver dollar
Lovely as a lily
Curious as a puppy
Alluring as a pinup
Sharp as a scalpel
Bold as brass
Sweet as maple sugar
Neat as a pin
Clean as a whistle
Friendly as a poodle
Well-coiffed as a diva
Skillful as a seamstress
Soft-hearted as a grape
Charming as a princess
Endearing as a forehead kiss
Intriguing as a French accent
Captivating as dimples
Independent as a lioness
Stubborn s a mule
Talkative as a magpie
Happy as a lark
Feminine as a woman should be
Loving as only a mother can be.
So Lucille Dolores is all of the above—
And much more, too!

I have just run out of words
to describe all of her
beguiling attributes and persona.
So, she has to know and understand
why and how much she is admired and loved
by everyone, including me.
HAPPY BIRTHDAY!

For Else-Marie on Christmas 2012

Another year has passed —
one that enhanced, enlarged, and encircled
both our continuing and growing love
for each other —
and included new and enduring health
and other challenges
for us to face, endure, and overcome.
Yet today is also a time for sharing,
a time for giving, and a time for believing
in the humanity and goodness of others,
including strangers, neighbors, friends, and family.
May the comfort and happiness you gave to me
and many others all year long
be returned to you now and in future years.
May Christmas love and peace fill your heart
and bless everyone and everything you hold dear
and then shine brightly on your way
through a joyous, rewarding, and happy New Year,
for Clarence, Kiana, yourself,
and others that you hold dear.
So, here is wishing you a holiday season
and a New Year filled with warmth,,
happiness, much love,
and memories to treasure all year long.

For Laine and Ben
On Their Engagement

This is the beginning of an important phase of your lives.
You'll always remember this momentous occasion.
Remarkably and most appropriately,
it began the traditional way
when Ben asked Sam, his prospective father-in-law,
for permission to ask the crucial query —
and received an immediate and positive response.
I assume that Ben, in turn, posed the question,
on bended knee to Laine,
Will you marry me?
And she ardently and tearfully accepted.
That question and answer mark the beginning
of a new and very different relationship
for it contains the promise that you both intend
to share fully your love and your life.
You have given each other
one of the greatest gifts that anyone can give —
total love and promise of mind, body, and soul.
Your family, relatives, and friends celebrate with you
on this most propitious of days.
And wish for you
every blessing that God and your loved ones
can grant or request,
among them, long and productive lives,
good health and fitness, joy and happiness,
and everything that will be useful to you
in your and God's plans.
May He watch over you, this day and always.
Love and felicitations.
September 12, 2012

For Else-Marie on Her 73rd Birthday

I know how badly life has treated you in recent years
and how difficult your physical problems have been:
The breast cancer, the colon cancer,
your chemo and radiation therapies, your surgeries,
your eye problems, hip replacement, and broken collarbone.
You are such a sweet, good-hearted, loving,
and lovable woman most of the time.
Those are happy days! I love being with you,
even when you are just lying on the couch
in the living room reading one of your novels —
even when you are in my den watching TV.
I also love conversing with you
and sharing memories of the last 12 years.
I enjoy making salads and cooking for you,
But I especially value the special times when we made love.
I pray every night, and have for about eight years,
for a cure for your cancers, control of your eye problems,
possible colon corrective surgery.
and a long, rewarding, and happy life
with your son, Clarence, and your granddaughter, Kiana.
I love you very much
and thank you for making the last 12 years
memorable, rewarding, and largely happy ones.
I wish that I could stay here with you for many more years.
But, as you can easily see, I cannot.
I am rapidly deteriorating, and I regret that.
However, no matter what, I shall be with you in spirit
and trust that we shall be together for eternity in Heaven
with our family members, friends, and lovers
who have passed on before us.
I wish you a happy birthday
and many more years of comfort and happiness.

I Had a Dream Last Night

I dream every night, but I often cannot recall the dream.
The nighttime visions and fantasies I remember
are often alarming and frightening.
A few are ordinary and commonplace,
all about mundane events.
Rarely, I have a dream that is very different
out of the ordinary, and s truly memorable.

Last night I had an extraordinary dream,
I was in my early 40s, visiting Tokyo, Japan on a
mission for an Army intelligence agency.
I was taking an after-dinner walk through
the Ginza District, the well known upscale shopping
area with numerous department stores,
boutiques, restaurants, and coffeehouses.

Ginza is recognized as one of the most luxurious
shopping districts in the world—
always crowded with Japanese people,
and foreign visitors, young, adolescent, and old,
strolling through the buildings teeming with people.

As I leisurely walked through a crowded arcade,
I saw a slender and lovely Caucasian lady, in her mid-20s,
with dark brown hair, peaches and cream complexion,
and a beguiling smile on her face,
wearing a beautiful dress, silk stockings, classic high-heel
pumps, and surrounded by an aura of
Prince Matchabelli Wind Song perfume.
She was walking through the arcade alone—
and looking very much lost.
In an instant, I decided that I just had to speak with her,

although I didn't know her.
I approached her and asked, "May I help you?"
She looked me straight in the eyes and to my surprise,
she smiled slightly, and in a soft, melodious voice,
and to my complete astonishment, she replied,
"No thanks, but I love you, Bill."

I immediately and enthusiastically embraced her and,
holding her close but not too tightly,
I kissed her pillow-soft lips slowly and lightly,
enjoying the sensation of warmth, innocence,
and unconditional love for about 20 seconds —
and then replied, "I love you, too!"

I released her, backed away slowly, said "Thank you,"
ok her hand in one of mine, encircled her waist with the other,
and started walking with the crowd of shoppers.

That's precisely when the dream ended,
nd I awakened with a profound feeling of complete happiness
—but only for a moment or two when I began
to feel a deep sense of loss.
I sincerely hope that I can repeat again and again
that nighttime piece of Heaven.

Haiku

A dream about love
Can be surprisingly real
But never lasts long

For Some Very Special Ladies

I have had scores of platonic relationships
with women of all cultures, ages, and careers—
babysitters, teachers, college professors, Army officers,
mentors, colleagues, friends, and acquaintances
—and many female relatives, aunts, cousins, and in-laws
I also had four sisters, two daughters, one spouse,
As well as several short-term dating relationships.
There were, however, only five close relationships
that had permanent and irrevocable effects
on me for the rest of my life.

First, my biological mother, Pauline Eva,
who died in childbirth, leaving six children,
including my new sister— and me at 16 months of age.
Second, my foster mother, Josephine Mary,
my mother's sister, who loved and cherished me,
as though she were my birth mother—
and made me the man I am today—
at least the positives of my character.
Third, my first true love, Lucille Dolores,
the girl with the musical voice,
the ready laugh, the warm persona—
the perfect and peerless dance partner.
Although I have not seen her
for more than 60 years
(the last time at a high school reunion dance)
I have never forgotten our teenage romance
and our dates at the Totem Pole ballroom
at Norumbega Park on the Charles River in Auburndale.
Fourth, my wife, Kathleen, mother of our six children,
who loved me totally and unconditionally,
despite my faults, shortcomings, and failings.

Fifth, my loving companion, Else-Marie Bowe,
who has given freely and consistently
her time, concern, help, affection, and love
to an irascible and temperamental old fogy.

I close this magnum opus
with a brief Valentine's Day declaration:
Ladies, all of you, including those unnamed,
occupy a special place in my heart,
as well as in the story of my life—
for the dates and fun times we shared,
and for the warmest wishes within my heart—
happiness for you and Happy Valentine's Day!

For Else-Marie II

I've tried to find the perfect words
To tell you how much you're loved—
But words that powerful and inspired
are all too few.
When a woman as stunning
and cherished as you are,
then all there is to say is…I love you.
So, you are a wonderful gift,
and my life is richer and better
because you're in it.
My feelings for you are always there
warm in my heart.
And I must thank you:
For everything you are to me
For everything you have done,
And for everything you continue to do.
You're really someone special
for everything you are to me…

For Laine on Her 29th Birthday

Today is your day!
Some lucky people just glow with life,
radiate warmth and love,
and make the world better
for everyone around them.
And you are blessed
to be one of the chosen.

So, there is no better day than this one
to celebrate and be grateful for YOU—
your beauty, your talents,
your kindness, your positive outlook,
and your helpfulness.
But, most important of all
to be the person
who makes every day
a lot better for all who know you
by just being YOU!

So, always remember
how important and how much
you are loved
by your family and friends.
So, I hope your birthday is the beginning
of a year of continuing success,
glittering opportunities,
and an abundance of happiness
for both you and Ben.
Love, Poppi

An Overpowering Need

When you love someone,
a person you see infrequently,
you have an all-consuming need
to do something for her often
so that you will not be forgotten.
You give her gifts that you hope
will touch her heart
and make her think of you.
Those small gifts
Would be given daily
If that were possible,
But it rarely is possible.
So you settle
for long or short messages
that you hope will
engage her interest and attention.
Occasionally you send a gift
of more permanent value,
such as a prayer,
a piece of jewelry,
a photo, book, video, or a verse.
And rarely, the most important event
of your month or longer,
you take her to lunch or dinner.
Those little presents are ways of saying,
in an indirect and different way,
I love you.
If you're lucky, you are rewarded
with hug and a chaste kiss.

Lucille

Today is your 90th birthday-
Despite the 70+ years since we last saw each other.
we have always been *More Than Friends*.
I have many precious memories of 1941.
I keep those memories *In a Very Special Place*.
Because, as long as I live, you will always be
My First Love.
Due to that unique position,
I Still Love You,
because of a first love it can truly be said,
Love Is Forever.
The First Time I Ever Saw Your Face,
was at Dolly McDaid's School of Dancing.
Then Came You into my life.
It was then that I said,
for the first of countless times,
Let's Dance!
Time After Time
that was *The Way We Were*,
and I was always *Close to You*.
In addition, I often told you
that *All I Want* is that you
Save the Last Dance for Me.
I have rarely been *On the Street Where You Live,*
but you have been *Always on My Mind*
Although I have not had an opportunity to see you
in person for many years,
Have I Told You Lately
that *You Are My Sunshine*
and that *I Will Always Love You*
Just the Way You Are?

I am now charmed, delighted, and enchanted
to have you as a close friend and confidant
because *You Light Up My Life*.
In 1941 everything was
Some Kind of Wonderful.
Although it may be true
It's Only Make Believe and that
We Are Never Ever Getting Back Together,
it is equally true that
You've Got a Friend forever.
So lets *Rock Around the Clock*,
Be-Bop-A-Lu
like *Great Balls of Fire*.
And be *Happy Together*
Somewhere
although we're far apart.
So, *Stand By Me.*
Reach Out I'll Be There.
HAPPY BIRTHDAY!

*****

Note: This poem uses the actual titles
of love songs.
published mainly in the 1940s.
Those titles appear in bold italics
in the preceding verse.

Haiku

A sweet and warm girl
Is a blessing from Above
Cherish and protect her.

My Special Gifts

Throughout my life I've received
many gifts that I hold dear.
Those blessings include
the people who loved me and are no longer here—
my parents, foster parents, and parents-in-law,
my wife of more than 53 years,
and my four sisters and three brothers.

But the greatest gift I have ever received
in all my days
is the one great gift made up of separate parts,
every one an individual gift
and each one securely resting in my heart.
This is the gift that made my life complete,
and at every thought of that beneficence
my heart skips a beat.

That gift is one that God sent to me —
one that is perfect and uniquely mine.
It is my family: my six children,
twelve grandchildren,
and three great grandchildren—
blessings that God has given to me.
But, for whatever the reason,
and known only to God and not to me.

There is one element of that gift
that has been closest to me —
one who must go nameless.
For to diminish in any way
my love for any of the others
would be tactless and unpardonable

and I hope that all my relationships
with all of the others
would allow any one of them
to say with complete certainty,
"That's me."

Our Family

God made us a family.
We work together and play together.
We need each other and love each other.
So we ask God to bless
the family we love
and comfort us each day.
As daytime turns into nighttime,
please, God, bring us peace, we pray.
When morning becomes tomorrow,
let all our cares be small,
and guide us with your wisdom.
Lord, bless us one and all.
Amen!

Haiku

Family must be first
In our actions and prayers
To be fulfilled

My Special Gardens

I have three special gardens
that blossom and thrive inside me.
The first contains two lovely daisies
and four handsome carnations
that I treasure with all my heart.
They are the best gifts God has given to me,
ones that I would never change for anything:
My six children, my precious offspring,
Bill Jr., Kevin, Brian, Kathy, Maura, and Sean.
They are the first garden in my life.

My second garden contains eight lovely daisies
and four handsome carnations,
grandchildren that mean the world to me:
Eight girls, Tamra, Jackie, Mikie, Laine,
Katie, Kolby, Kaylyn, and Siara,
And four boys, Sean, Will, Tim, and Victor.

My third garden, my great grandchildren
is not yet complete,
for it contains only two gardenias —
two girls, Kaila and Grace
and one carnation, David.
With time and God's beneficence,
there are certainly more blossoms to come.

I'll be with all of my gardens until God takes me.
They are now the reason for my existence,
the incentive for my everyday life.
Every day I feed and water my plants with prayers
so they can grow straight and healthy.

Thoughts, Wishes, and Prayers
for My Grandchildren and Great Grandchildren

Here are my beliefs about
The most important things in life:
Have realistic, achievable, and worthwhile goals.
Find your real talents, the things you like and do best.
Every one has one or more.
The challenge is to identify them.

Commit to learning, mastering, and burnishing
the skills and knowledge needed
to make the most of those talents.
Be persistent in the pursuit of your goals.
Never be satisfied that you have achieved perfection.
Work at the job without tiring or yielding to adversity.

Always remember the importance of family —
Revere your ancestors on both sides of your family,
your parents and grandparents, siblings, aunts and uncles,
and cousins — their talents, accomplishments,
and the rich heritage they have left to you
or now share with you.
Love them for what and who they are or were,
and show them that you love them.

Here are my wishes for you:
That you find and exploit your God-given talents.
That you honor your heritage and your family.
And, finally, here are my prayers for you:
That you have a long, healthy, happy, and rewarding life.
That you find a true soul mate and together
have healthy and happy children.
That you exemplify the values of love of God and
compassion and charitableness toward all others.

Kay Is for Kathleen

Never a "Kay" in appearance, temperament, or personality.
Those words never fit you,
one who is invariably soft, nurturing, and loving,
never one who is hard, cynical, or negative.

When we first met,
I was an unhappy, insecure young man,
A person with self-doubts and low self-esteem.
You cured my weaknesses by giving me
support, and unfailing, unstinting love.

My memories span more than fifty-two years.
Our first date was at Fitchburg State —
The Winter Carnival Ball —
the night I told you that I was going to marry you.

Meeting you at the Oakland train station,
when I returned to the States from the Pacific War.
Saying goodbye to you at the San Francisco Embarcadero,
Meeting you a year later at the Worcester train station
when I came home after the war ended.

Visiting you at the Lucy Helen Maternity Hospital
following the births of Bill Jr., Kevin, Brian,
Kathy, and Maura — and then Sean at the Burbank Hospital
So many wonderful memories!

Not enough people know how selfless and giving
you have been all your life.
Your kindness, thoughtfulness, and caring
did not stop with our children and grandchildren
Your love was freely given to many others.

I remember what you did for Susie Gurley,
Rosie O'Grady, Charlotte Mann, Mildred Hawes, and Peg
McCormick —and for your Aunt Margareeta,
Aunt Maime, Uncle Cecil —
and for the hundreds of kids in your classrooms
over the years —
the regular kids, the kids with retardation, the delinquents,
and the kids in Religions Education classes.

You have given much to me and to many others.
Your greatest gift to all of us has been your total and
unconditional love.
So, Kathleen, thank you for being you,
my supporter, my partner, and my lover.

Marrying you was the smartest and best thing
I have ever done in my whole life.
I am a very lucky man!
Thank you from the bottom of my heart
on our 50th anniversary.

Haiku

A perfect truism
Love rules without any rules
Retain that always

Love is in the heart
Not in the circumstances
Recognize that fact

Two Lives

It happened almost 18 years ago,
And now it's over.
Our lives are now quite different
in more ways than one.
You went one way,
and I went mine.
Yet, someday I hope
our paths will again intertwine.
That I loved you very much,
I could never deny.
You were the beautiful girl
I let into my life.
With you, I shard my memories,
my hopes, and my dreams.
But then I discovered
that you would share
very few of yours with me.
I really don't understand
that what I did was so wrong.
Please tell me why
so that I can now carry on.

Family

The center of life
Is a loving family
Earned, never issued

For Katie on Her 20th Birthday

I regret that we have not been in contact
in the last few years despite my notes
and the two brief recent phone conversations.
I especially appreciated the most recent call
and look forward to your visit with your boy friend.
Nonetheless, I find it difficult to understand
why you have failed to acknowledge
the high school graduation,
Christmas, and birthday gifts.
It takes very little time, at most a few minutes,
to write a note or make a quick phone call.
By way of contrast, I take upwards of three hours
to compose, revise, mount on greeting cards,
and mail individual verses
for the birthdays of each of my children,
their spouses, my grandchildren and their spouses,
my great grandchildren, and many close friends.
— a total of about 80 verses
and more than 200 hours of work each year.
That series of events, except your impending visit,
is history or water over the dam.
Let us start anew the loving relationship
of earlier years.
I miss them and look forward to their return.
I leave this epistle with much love,
my heart-felt nightly prayers, best wishes,
and this Irish Blessing:
May God be with you and Bless you.
May you be poor in misfortunes
and rich in blessings.
May you know nothing but happiness
from this day forward.

For Kolby on Her 16th Birthday

Now this is really a big,
propitious, and auspicious day.
In most of the United States,
you are now eligible to take the exam
for a driver's license.
After successfully passing the written
and "behind the wheel" tests,
you will then have new freedom
as well as serious responsibilities—
always to obey the law,
the rules of the road,
and to drive carefully and attentively.

I also know that the past year has been
a very difficult one for you,
I know that you have been undeservedly
maligned, criticized, and mistreated, even bullied,
on numerous occasions.
Believe me, your Poppi knows what that
is like and what it can do to you.
That is because I was tormented by my foster father
from the age of six or eight until I left
for combat service in the Pacific War in 1943.
Ed Tracey repeatedly told me
that I was stupid, that I would never amount to anything,
that I was useless, and that I was a loser.
The bullying was incessant
and continued until my first trip home from the war,
with my ensign's insignia, combat ribbons,
and two battle stars.

Pop Tracey couldn't wait to take me around
to his barroom haunts to introduce "his son"
to his drinking buddies.

From that time on, my foster father accepted me.
Why did he persecute me so much and for so many years?
First, he was an alcoholic
and died some years later with that disease.
He was also very jealous of my foster mother's
love of me and her valiant and continuing
efforts to rear me properly,
allow me to retain my ambition and self-confidence,
and love me unconditionally.
If I had allowed Ed Tracey to destroy my dreams
and thwart my ambitions,
I would not have gone to college and graduate school,
become a teacher and professor, and later in my career,
a successful manager and international consultant—
or even a writer of 14 professional books and
four (going on five) books of poetry.

So, remember this:
You are a smart, bright, beautiful, and accomplished
young woman with a great future as a
successful professional (you fill in the occupation),
and an exemplary wife and mother.
Never let your unfortunate experiences
in recent years get you down.
Your Dad, sister, aunts and uncles, cousins, friends,
and grandfather will be with you always
and never let you down.
You can count on them!

HAPPY BIRTHDAY!

For Kevin on His 65th Birthday

At the prime and noteworthy age of 65,
you can count your many blessings.
Among the most important
are your wife, Lin, daughters, Kolby and Kaylyn,
your brothers and sisters, your many friends,
and your good health.
So, although your have only lived
about 71 percent of the number of years
with which I have been blessed to reach,
you remain in good health and physical shape
(although you really need to lose a few pounds)
your mental acuity remains robust, and your
sexual interest, capabilities, and prowess (I'm told)
remain intact and top-notched, even unmatched!
So, if you continue with a well-balanced diet
and a regular fitness/exercise routine,
you should easily exceed my record of longevity.
To achieve that goal,
as well as continue feeling alive and relevant,
I also highly recommend that you continue
to surround yourself with young people
as often and as much as possible.
Your daughters, nieces, and nephews
can provide much of that contact
and contribute to the fulfillment of that need.
Of course, Lin will always be a wellspring
of youthful perspectives and activities for you.
I trust that you and she will take full advantage
of that all-important resource.
Here is my aspiration for you and Lin:
My wish is as big as all outdoors
And that the best things in life will always be yours.

I close with this Irish blessing:
May your mornings bring joy,
And your evenings bring peace.
May your troubles grow few
And your blessings increase.
With much pride and love.

Saint Valentine's Day

People celebrate Valentines day on 14th February.
The day was first associated with romantic love
in the High Middle Ages,
when the tradition of courtly love flourished.
In 18th-century England, it evolved into an occasion
in which lovers expressed their love for each other
by presenting or sending flowers, confections,
and greeting cards known as "*valentines*."
It is now the traditional day on which people
express their love by sending cards, flowers,
typically, mixed flowers or red roses,
or candy, usually boxes of chocolates.
Only a few people compose their own cards
with an appropriate verse inscribed thereon.
Valentine's Day symbols used today
include the heart-shaped outline,
doves, and the figure of the winged Cupid.
Since the 19th century, handwritten valentines
have been replaced by mass-produced greeting cards.
In the 1980s, the diamond industry began
to promote Valentine's Day
as an occasion for giving jewelry.
pproximately 190 M valentines are sent each year in the US.

For Brian on His 65th Birthday

At the prime and notable age of 65,
you can count your many blessings.
Among the most important:
your wife, Joanne, daughters, Jackie and Mikie,
your grandchildren, Grace and David,
your brothers and sisters, your many friends,
and your good health.
So, although you have only lived
about 71 percent of the number of years
with which I have been blessed to reach,
you remain in good health and physical shape,
your mental acuity remains robust. and
your sexual interest, capabilities, and prowess (I'm told)
remain intact, top-notch, and unmatched.
So, if you continue maintaining a well-balanced diet
and a regular fitness/exercise routine.
you should easily exceed my record of longevity.
To achieve that goal,
as well as continue feeling alive and relevant,
I also highly recommend that you continue
to surround yourself with young people
as often and as much as possible.
Your daughters, grandchildren, and nieces and nephews
can provide much of that contact
and contribute to the fulfillment of that need.
Of course, Joanne will always be a wellspring
of youthful perspectives and activities for you.
I trust that she and you will take full advantage
of that all-important resource.
Here is my aspiration for you and your family:
my wish is as big as all outdoors,
and that the best things in life will always be yours!

I close with this Irish blessing:
May your mornings bring joy,
And your evenings bring peace.
May your troubles grow few
And your blessings increase.
Sincerely,
With much pride and love
Dad

Identical Twin Brothers

Guardian Angel, protect and guide
always by my side.
Brothers are always there,
with laughter, love, and care.

How blessed I am,
how fortunate I've been,
that your are my twin brother
and also my friend!

Brothers love, and brothers care.
Sometimes they disagree, but that's ok.
A twin brother is a special friend.
Forever family.

Brian, (this is Kevin) I'm smiling
because you are my twin brother
And I'm laughing because
there's nothing
you can do about it!

For Joanne on Her 64th Birthday

A life-long booster
of her handsome and talented rooster,
Brian John, father of Jackie and Mikie —
and grandfather of David and Gracie,
two of my twelve grandchildren
and two of my three great grandchildren.
So, she is not only a loving wife and mother,
but also a doting Nanna.
Joanne is also a frequent back seat passenger
of the Seattle-based Tracey Family's
classy Harley-Davidson Hog.
I first met that lovely chick when she was in her early 20s,
wearing her stylish Mohawk Air Line's
stewardess' (flight attendant's) uniform.
She has long been a top-notch candidate
for the role of female top banana,
or other inimitable and preeminent comedienne.
Ever loquacious and sometimes racy, even risqué,
she always says what she wants
and means what she says.
She invariably exemplifies that old but true maxim:
A friend in need is a friend indeed.
To sum it up, Joanne is not only my daughter-in-law,
she always has been, and still remains, my friend.
It is difficult for me to describe
how much Joanne means to me
because she means so much.
So, all that I can do now is tell her something
that I have never said to her before:
I LOVE YOU
and hope that those three words say it all.

My Brother, John Joseph

Jack was the second son of my Dad
and Sally McNamara O'Neill.
He was born December 26, 1934 in Leominster.
and married Sandra Goland October 9, 1966;
They had three daughters, Mary Ellen, Margaret,
and Elizabeth Ann.
Jack was one of the brightest of the O'Neill clan.
He held high-salaried positions as shipping manager
for several large corporations, including Sylvania
on Route 28, just outside of Boston.
After serving his enlistment in the Army on Okinawa,
where he probably developed his reliance on alcohol,
Jack returned to pursue his business career.
Unfortunately, following my adoption as a Tracey,
Jack never accepted me and my failure to change my name
back to O'Neill when my adoptive parents died.
Jack was an O'Neill to the core and believed
that it was unacceptable for any O'Neill to give up
his birth name and heritage —
especially someone who had achieved
recognition and some success in an honorable profession.
I deeply regret that Jack disowned me
and that he died in the way that he did.

Haiku

Take care of yourself
There is only one of you
And no duplicates

For Katie on Her 21st Birthday

Today is very important
because it signifies the age at which
a girl becomes a woman,
with all the privileges and responsibilities
that status allows or demands.
Although the age qualification
may seem to be of paramount importance,
it is not nearly as significant
or portentous as others.
The changes that began with puberty
are not just monumental
and imposing but also conspicuous,
wondrous, and striking
because they have changed the total you —
Katie and Kathleen Elizabeth — your mind,
body, persona, interests, needs, perspective,
objectives, and life goals —
in short, your whole, unique self,
including your morals, ethics, and character.
So, what do I need, want, and expect
from my bright and beautiful granddaughter?
First and foremost,
I want her to remain a <u>good</u> person
in every sense of the word —
a good and loving daughter, sister, granddaughter,
cousin, friend, acquaintance, and neighbor —
and later, a good and loving spouse, mother, aunt,
even grandmother and great grandmother.
Although there are many prescriptions
for success in life,
Regardless of profession, occupation, or calling,

I have one that I have
recommended to my children
and my students at all levels
from grade and high school, through military schools
to graduate schools.
I call them the seven keys to success
in whatever you do in life.
Here they are:

COMMITMENT
— to your family, organization and its mission,
— and to personal excellence
COMPETENCE
— in performing personal, technical, and managerial tasks
CONCERN
— for people, superiors, peers, subordinates;
— and especially for children
CONFIDENCE
— in oneself, superiors, peers, and subordinates
CONTROL
— self-control, the ability to function under pressure,
to avoid display of impatience, anxiety, or bad temper
COURAGE
— physical bravery, but of more importance, moral valor
CREDIBILITY
— being believable and enabling people to have
full confidence in your integrity

HAPPY BIRTHDAY!

For Frank on His 70th Birthday

I confess that I'm baffled, confused, and bewildered
about my motives for wanting
to communicate with you —
or even wanting to wish you a happy birthday.
I do know that I am truly and deeply disappointed,
yes, even dismayed and disheartened,
by your failure to acknowledge receipt of my phone calls,
letters, birthday cards, and invitations to my wife's
annual cemetery visits, anniversary Masses,
and family dinners.
So, I have heard nothing from my nephew
for several years— actually since your mother's funeral.
From my perspective, a widowed 91-year old
father of six, grandfather of 13,
and great grandfather of three,
has always been a person
who considers family contacts and interactions
the most important and potentially satisfying
relationships a person can have in a lifetime.
I wonder if you remember
your visits to Townsend, Fitchburg, Cape Cod, Manchester,
Hollis, and Bedford with your Mom?
My personal background (losing my mother
at age 16 months when my sister, Eileen, was born),
deprived of frequent contact with my father,
adopted by a loving aunt Josephine,
and later renewing contacts with my older brother, Jim,
and my sisters Mary, Pauline, and Margaret,
and my new brothers, Frank and Jack,
made me more conscious and convinced
of the importance, the criticality, of family.

I wish that you would recognize that fact,
that truth, that reality.
That's why I'm writing to you now —
five months ahead of your natal day—
what I really want to communicate to you.
This could probably be my last communication.
Please give me a phone call!
HAPPY BIRTHDAY

Haiku

Feel good about now
It's a very special time
Enjoy it fully

Take care of yourself
Enjoy healthful food and drink
Live a lengthy life

Those who bring sunshine
Into the lives of others
Earn it for themselves

Discover yourself
Know who you really are now
Apply what you have learned

Daydream regularly
To loose creativity
Is a disaster

Smile before sleeping
You will slumber more soundly
And dream much better

For Ben on His 28th Birthday

"Big" Ben and "The Gentle Giant"
are appropriate sobriquets or monikers
for my new grandson–in-law,
now the husband of my granddaughter, Laine.
Yes, Ben is king-size,
a really big dude—
six feet three, 210 pounds,
and wears size 13 shoes
and 44L jackets.
In my Cape Cod house, with its seven foot ceilings.
six foot hanging ceiling fans,
and six and one-half foot doorways
he has to be very cautious.
And, of course, he is kind in manner
toward friend and stranger,
young and old, and human and animal.
Ben is, by nature, quiet, amiable, approachable,
helpful, kindhearted, reliable,
and friendly, but is, at the same time,
always self-controlled, reserved, and self-reliant.
Most of the foregoing traits and qualities
are easily observable.
However, there are many other facts about his lineage,
talents, and accomplishments
that casual contact would not reveal about Ben.
Here are a few examples:
His pride in his Tlingit Alaskan Native
Tribal Heritage and Culture.
His respect for and appreciation of his Dad's
honorable military service and accomplishments

as a senior noncommissioned officer
in the United States Air Force
in the Grade of Master Sergeant, E-7.
His achievement in attaining the status of
an elite level of play in both singles and doubles
as a tennis team member throughout his college career
and holding Junior Regional Ranking
in the Pacific Northwest US Tennis Association.
His B.S. in Computer Science and Cyber Security
following completion of only three more courses.
His skills as a bowler and a Zumba dancer.
His hobby of collecting comic books,
such as Batman, Wolverine, Superman,
Wonder Woman, and Black Widow.
I close with this bit of verse:
May your day be touched
By a bit of Tlingit luck,
Brightened by a song in your heart.
And warmed by the smiles
Of the people you love,
including Bentley.
HAPPY BIRTHDAY!
From your Grandfather-in-Law

Haiku

Wishing you always
Lots of laughter to cheer you
And your love near you

Build a joyful place
For both you and your true love
Live there forever

For Mikie on Her 35th Birthday

This day marks another milestone
in your life journey.
And for your Poppi, December 29, 2014
will document an astonishing accomplishment,.
his 92nd natal day
(assuming that he will still be here.)
As an old saying plaintively notes,
Whether you're ready or not,
time marches on.
But, this bit of verse is about and for you,
my beautiful, signally entrepreneurial, talented,
and accomplished granddaughter—
one of whom I remember every night
as I say my bedtime prayers,
when I ask God
to keep you well, safe, content, and happy
in your love life
as well as in your professional endeavors.
My fervent wish for you:
that you are blessed with the gifts
that God gave to your Nanni and me —
three years of truly romantic courtship,
53 years of sharing true love and happiness.
and the special gifts of six wonderful children,
12 beautiful and talented grandchildren,
and three bewitching great grandchildren.
Unfortunately, Nanni did not live long enough
to meet and enjoy our grandchildren,
Victor, Kolby, Kaylyn, and Siara,
or our great grandchildren,
Kaila, Grace, and David.

But I'm certain that she is watching them with love
from her perch high in Heaven.
I close this verse in true Irish vernacular:
May the saints protect ye,
An' sorrow neglect ye,
An' bad luck t' the one
That doesn't respect ye.
An' the top of the morning
T' all that belong t' ye,
An' long life t' yer honour;
That's the end of my song t' ye!
HAPPY BIRTHDAY!

Haiku

May you have warm words
On a very cold evening
And a safe path home

Wishing you always
Strong walls for the Western wind
And tea near the fire

May you always have
Good luck to make you smile
And plenty of love

Keep a list of dreams
That you hope will come to pass
Instead of bad ones

For David on His 3rd Birthday

Your Great Poppi had seven siblings,
your great uncles and aunts —
three brothers, from oldest to youngest,
Jim, Frank, and Jack,
and four sisters, also from eldest to youngest,
Mary, Polly, Peggy, and Eileen.
I loved all of them very much,
but they are all in Heaven now.
The ones who were closest to me,
were the eldest of each gender,
Jim and Mary, both of whom were very special —
Jim, because we were close in age
and spent lots of time together over many years,
and Mary because she was my big sister,
who taught me a lot of very important things
and took me on several big trips,
including New York City.
We visited Rockefeller Center, saw the Rockettes,
had dinner at Toffinetti's restaurant on Times Square,
visited Jack Dempsey's eatery, where I shook hands
with the former World's Heavyweight Boxing Champion,
had breakfast at the Automat,
climbed to the top of the Statue of Liberty,
toured the Hall of Fame at New York University,
visited Grant's Tomb, and stopped by other tourist attraction
I mention those people and places
because sisters and brothers are so important —
and you are lucky to have an older sister, Gracie.
She can teach you a lot of useful things,
and, more important, because you are her younger brother,
she will always love you and be there for you —

as you must always love her and be there for her forever..
So remember this about Gracie, your big sister:
There is but one and only one,
Whose love will fail you never.
One who lives from sun to sun,
With constant fond endeavor.
There is but one and only one,
On earth there will be no other,
with the exception of your mother,
When God gave you a big sister.
Who will love you forever.
HAPPY BIRTHDAY!

Note: I hope that your Grandfather and/or your Dad
will read this verse to you AND that, when you are older,
you will read it again.

A Gaelic Christening Blessing

Dearest Father in Heaven
Bless this child
and bless this day
of new beginnings.
Smile upon this child
and surround this child, Lord,
with the soft mantle of Your love.
Teach this child to follow
in Your footsteps and to live life
in the ways of love,
faith, hope, and charity.

For Joanne on Her 65th Birthday

It's time for another verse; this time using song titles
that are familiar to you
because they were popular *Yesterday,*
when you were a *Pretty (young) Woman*
the equivalent of a *Surfer Girl* in California.
Do You Want to Know A Secret?
It's certainly not *Hanky Panky,*
nor am I *Goin' Out of My Head'*
It's simply that I'm intrigued, entertained, and mystified
by *The Way You Do the Things You Do.*
It's clear to everyone
that by no stretch of the imagination
is it true that at age 91+, *Time Is On My Side.*
And that's ok with me, because it's not
The End of The World; I can *Walk Right In* and sing
Zip-A-Dee Doo-Dah.
In fact, it's probable that the two of us
could *Walk On By* and *Sing in the Sunshine.*
But, let me be serious for a moment.
I'm Telling You Now, and *It's Not Unusual*
to *Stop in the Name of Love*
and *I'll Never Find Another You.*
I also need to tell you, *Just Once in My Life*
that *I Love You Because,* in Sonny Bono's words,
I Get You Babe and *I'm Telling You Now*
because it is your natal day— and also because
What the World Needs Now Is Love
And that *Our Day Will Come!*
I also need to remind you
that in my status as your father-in-law
you should take this advice seriously:
Don't Mess With Bill.
Love,
There I've Said It Again

What Is a Grandfather?

A grandfather is a man who has
lived a lot of years,
seen and done a lot of things,
but has also shed a lot of tears.
Although he's had a long life,
not too long from today,
he will join his loving wife.
He's your Nanni's spouse,
and your Mom's or Dad's daddy.
But to Tamra, Sean, Jackie, Mikie,
Laine, and LB, Tim. Katie,
Kolby and Kaylyn, he's simply Poppi —
and to Kaila, Grace, and David,
he is Great Poppi.
And to Victor and Siara, he is Abuelo.
But most of all,
He's a man who loves his family,
who is proud of whom they are
and what they have done.
He also hopes and prays
that some day they will have
children, grandchildren,
and great grandchildren
of their own
to love and make him proud!

For My Grandson WRT III on His 27th Birthday

I confess that I have been baffled, confused, and bewildered
about my motives for wanting
to communicate with you —
or even wanting to wish you a happy birthday.
I do know that I am truly and deeply disappointed.
yes, even dismayed and disheartened,
by your failure to acknowledge receipt of my Christmas
and birthday gifts and verses (with a few exceptions)
over the last 20+ years — but even more
by your failure to respond to my request that you
let me know that you received
two of my prized possessions:
my enlisted and commissioned officer Navy
identification bracelets, one gold and the other silver,
that I mailed to you several months ago.
From my perspective, a widowed 91-year old
father of six, grandfather of 13,
and great grandfather of three,
has always been a person
who considers family contacts and interactions
the most important and potentially satisfying
relationships a person can have in a lifetime.

With the exception of details about your current situation
and plans for the future,
that is now all water-over-the-dam— explained by your
emails of July 8 and 15.
However, I repeat my reaction to your notes in my return
missive of July 11:
I thank you for your notes and now understand your reluctan
to contact me — and I'm not surprised by the underlying
reasons for your behavior.

Yes, we do need to talk more about that as soon
as we can get together
—not vindictively or punishment in any sense,
but to show affection and provide whatever help I can.

I wonder if you remember
the Easter egg hunts at Cape Cod
and Manchester with your Nanni and me?
Or the Christmases and other holidays at the Cape,
Portsmouth, Manchester, Bedford, and Hollis?
And I recall with deep pride, attending a performance of
Macbeth, starring Kelsey Grammer and my talented grandson
in Boston —
and also viewing the TV show you starred in
some years ago.
Do you remember your Nanni's and my attendance
at the old and new churches in Manchester
where you were a server at Mass?
My personal background (losing my mother
at age 16 months when my sister, Eileen, was born),
deprived of frequent contact with my father,
adopted by a loving aunt Josephine,
and later renewing contacts with my older brother, Jim,
and my sisters Mary, Pauline, and Margaret,
and my new brothers, Frank and Jack,
made me more conscious and convinced
of the importance, the criticality, of family.
I wish that you would recognize that fact,
that truth, that reality.
That's why I'm writing to you now —
what I really want to communicate to you.
HAPPY BIRTHDAY!

For Maura on Her 60th Birthday

It's hard to believe that
my little blonde Peanut
has lived six decades of a productive,
out-of-the-ordinary and interesting life.

As a child and adolescent, Maura was
blonde in coloring and light in spirit.
A practiced and frequent top-of-the-refrigerator sitter
and a Bimbo conspirator and sharer of checkups,
her Dad's frequent late night visitor and TV watcher,
Kathy's collaborator in cluttering their bedroom and
Sean's Maw-Maw and on-the-hip transportation.

She was also an inveterate picky (or eclectic) eater,
the twins' secondary target for teasing and torment,
Bill Cabana's Girl Friday,
the Tracey Barn Circus' daring beam walker,
Mrs. Mann's nemesis and *tour de force*,
an unpredictable wanderer and explorer
and always a little mother.

As an adult, Maura was and is —
a self-reliant and independent woman,
an unwilling but accomplished scholar,
Steve's partner and helper,
a gifted teacher, coach and counselor,
a great cook — Italian or any other style,
an exemplary and thorough housekeeper,
a willing and fast worker at any job,
a "quick read" for anything new and different,

a "take charge" person for both planning and execution,
and Steve's perfect companion and greatest gift.
And daughter Laine's mentor and best friend,
a loving daughter, mother, sister, cousin, aunt and friend.
Born to be a boss!

I close with this wish and prayer:

May everything happy
and everything bright
be on your birthday
from morning 'til night,
And then through the year,
may the same thing hold true,
So that every day is filled
with God's blessings for you!
Have a Happy Birthday!

The Ten Greatest Blessings

Honest work to challenge and occupy you.
A hearty appetite to sustain and delight you.
A good man to love and care for you.
Children to love, teach and cherish for life.
Friends to support and help you when you are in need.
Good health and vigor to keep you active.
The time required to do the things you want to do.
A long, productive and interesting life.
A good, lasting, and permanent relationship with God.
And a wink from the Almighty to let you know that He is
always watching.

For Victor on His 16th Birthday

Some food for thought on this auspicious occasion—
truisms that you will understand and support —
even if your have never thought about them before.
So, although you may never
have given voice to these beliefs,
I hope that you know
that these axioms, platitudes, and maxims
are important facets of your being, your persona,
and your identity, when appropriately applied.
They also show the depth and strength of your character.
The fact that they are stated in *haiku*
makes them even more significant, weighty, and memorable

Haiku

Discover yourself
Who you are and want to be
When you reach your goals

You have a strong voice
Take positions on issues
Boldly and clearly

Do your very best
Even when no one watches
That marks competence

A generous man
Who restores others in need
Will himself be healed

My youngest grandson
A would-be starring point guard
I hope he makes it

The key to long life:
Stay positive in outlook
Don't sweat the small stuff

Understand this truth
You're better than you believe
Enjoy your blessings

Take care of yourself
There is only one of you
And no duplicates

Here are both a prayer and an Irish birthday wish
from your mostly-Irish grandfather:

Wherever you go
and whatever you do,
May the luck of your part-Irish heritage
be there with you.

Wishing you always
Walls for the wind,
A roof for the rain
And tea beside the fire.
Laughter to cheer you,
Those you love near you,
and all that your heart may desire.

HAPPY BIRTHDAY!

For Maura on Her 59th Birthday

You have lived through some very difficult years:
A marriage that was not going well, separation,
retirement, moves to Cape Cod
and then back to Rome,
a new love with a caring and superlative man
and now, a long-awaited wedding
for Laine with the right man.

In my view, Laine had three serious suitors:
The first (J) was an exploiter, user and loser,
and a seasoned manipulator.
The second (P) was self-centered.
domineering, and controlling.
The third suitor was and is dependable
He is unquestionably, Mr. Right —
a good and true man in every way.

To use a baseball metaphor,
Laine's first relationship (J) resulted in a foul ball
on the screen behind home plate.
The next liaison (P) produced a popup
that dropped into the left field seats.
The last and most significant affiliation (B)
produced a bases-clearing (Grand Slam) home run!

I am very happy with that outcome
and wish with all my heart
that I could be at that wedding.
Unfortunately, my age and poor health
will not allow that.
However, I shall be there in spirit!

For Maura Gail

In the past, I have often tried to find the perfect words
to tell you how much you're loved—
and let my second daughter know
how proud I am of her
despite the challenges
she has faced over the years.
Although I have often tried to find the perfect words
to say how much you're loved,
I have often been unable to voice them.
So, I have failed to tell you
how much it means to me to have a daughter like you,
to tell you about the joy that comes from being loved,
and the confidence that accrues to being respected
and believed in by my daughter.
It is difficult for me to describe how much you mean to me
because you mean so much.
So, all that I can do now is tell you something
that I have not said to you often enough:
I LOVE YOU
and hope that those three words say it all.

I close with this old Irish blessing

May the rains sweep gentle
across your fields,
May the sun warm the land,
May every good seed
you have planted bear fruit,
And late summer find you
standing in fields of plenty.

For Kevin on His 66th Birthday

So another year has passed —
and that period of time is a long and trying one
for more than one reason.
The first incident had both a good and bad outcome:
Kolby's move to your home —
where she is truly wanted
and loved by her Dad and her step-mother, Lin,
as well as by her sister, Kaylyn,
and her many close relatives and friends.

The negative side was her mother's
bullying and ultimate rejection of her daughter.
The second was the direct result
of a lethargic and staggering economy —
the fault of an incompetent chief executive
and a spiteful, do-nothing Congress —
an awful time to build a new business.
I am confident that your entrepreneurial skills
and steadfast and unremitting efforts
will be rewarded by
rapid growth and ultimate success
as the business environment improves.

My main concern about my number two son
is his physical and emotional health.
The former is the more important,
due mainly to the O'Neill family's
history of frequent heart attacks, strokes,
and early deaths — all of my father's brothers
and Dad himself were victims,
as well as my brother, Jim, and even me,

at age 91+ with AFIB, irregular heart rhythm,
and now nine years living
with daily heart medication and pacemakers.
So all of my children, but particularly my sons,
must be careful about their diet, their weight,
and regular monitoring of their hearts'
performance and condition.
Enough about those things.

Always remember that,
although I don't say it often,
I love you very much and am very proud
of your accomplishments over many years:
student, teacher, musician, entertainer, businessman,
entrepreneur, son, father, brother, cousin,
uncle, and friend.

I close with this old Irish prayer:
May the saints protect ye,
An' Heaven bless and keep ye,
An' bad luck t' the one
That doesn't respect ye,
An' the top of the mornin'
T' all that belong t' ye,
An' long life t' yer honour,
And that's the end of my verse t' ye!

≈

Haiku

Three essential traits
For success in any field
Smarts, grace, and wisdom

For Brian on His 66th Birthday

So another year has passed —
and that period was a long and rewarding one
for more than one reason.
The first reward was the growth and development
of your two beautiful grandchildren,
Grace Marie; and David Matthew,
I am fortunate to have lived long enough
to meet both of those bright, lovely
and handsome, comely and gracious,
and personable and loving successors.

The second notable was the direct result
of your entrepreneurship and business acumen.
You took full advantage of a rare opportunity
when you acquired Ride the Ducks of Seattle.
You then exercised outstanding management skills
by developing and expanding your holdings
into a highly successful business.

I am confident that your entrepreneurial skills
and steadfast and unremitting effort
will be rewarded by continued growth and success,
which you can proudly leave as an endowment
for your children and grandchildren.

My main concern about my number three son
is his physical health.
That element is of primary importance
mainly because of the O'Neill family's
history of frequent heart attacks,
strokes, and early deaths.

All of my father's brothers and Dad himself
were victims, as well as my brother, Jim,
my first cousin, General Jack O'Neill, and even me,
at age 91+ with AFIB, irregular heart rhythm,
living with daily heart medications and pacemakers.

So all of my children, but particularly my sons,
must be careful about their diet, their weight,
and regular monitoring of their hearts'
performance and condition.

Enough about those things.
Always remember that,
although I don't say it often,
I love you very much and am very proud
of your accomplishments over many years:
student, teacher, musician, entertainer,
radio and TV personality, businessman,
entrepreneur, son, father, brother, cousin,
uncle, and friend.

I close with this old Irish prayer:
May your day be touched
by a bit of Irish luck,
brightened by a song in your heart,
and warmed by the smiles
of the people you love.
And from now and tomorrow
to the end of your life
Be long and joyful.

A prayer for you.
A long, hale, and happy life
Truly lacking strife

For Jackie M. on Her 38th Birthday

April 9, 2014 was a very special day
for your grandfather: when I met,
for the very first time:
two of my three great grandchildren:
David Matthew Munson,
my active, 100 percent male, and only great grandson
And I also again greeted and hugged my
beautiful great granddaughter
after several years of no direct contact.
It meant so much to me because I feared
that our meeting would not happen.
So, I am grateful to you and Matt
for bringing them to visit me —
and also thankful that God has blessed me
by allowing an old man to live long enough
to meet Grace and David
as well as their cousin, Kaila Lee Lumpkin.
That fact is especially noteworthy
because not many great grandfathers are given
that very special privilege.
I learned that David has the personality,
as well as the demeanor and propensities, of his Dad—
and will retain them until late in his teens, if not longer.
That heritage will certainly in the next decade
be very interesting and exciting for you and Matt.
Grace is a real girl child— a lovely, dutiful.
and malleable little mother, and a joy to be around.
The two handwritten notes she gave me with hearts
and the words, "I love you Great Poppi" are precious
So, you and Matt are blessed with two
-striking, remarkable, and wonderful children
I wish I could be around to watch them grow and mature.

But that cannot happen.
Nevertheless, I shall be watching them with their Nanni,
God willing, from our perches in Heaven.
Here is a special Irish blessing for the Munson family:
May there always be work for your hands to do.
May your purse always hold a coin or two.
May the sun always shine on your windowpane.
May a rainbow be certain to follow each rain.
May the hand of a friend always be near you.
May God fill your heart with gladness to cheer you.
HAPPY BIRTHDAY!

For Laine and Ben

I don't know how, when, or where you met.
No matter, it was a fortuitous happening!
You were lucky to find each other,
even if your paths crossed only by chance.
And now your lives are intertwined in a relationship
that can only be described as a beautiful romance.
I can even picture what may have happened:
A chance meeting
became a smile, became a conversation,
became a touch, became a kiss,
became love, became a destiny,
became a commitment.
And now you are engaged to be married.
I could not be happier for you and for me too,
because I will soon be gaining a handsome, genial,
and loving grandson-in-law —
a perfect match for my beautiful, talented,
and affectionate granddaughter.
Congratulations and Best Wishes!

For David on His Fourth Birthday

April 9, 2014 was a very special day
for your great grandfather:
I met you, David Matthew Munson,
for the very first time!
It meant so much to me
because I feared that our meeting
would not happen.
So, I am grateful that God has blessed me
by allowing this old man to live long enough
to meet his only great grandson,
and also his two great granddaughters,
your sister, Grace Marie Munson,
and your cousin, Kaila Lee Lumpkin.
That fact is especially noteworthy
because not many great grandfathers are given
that very special privilege.

I am also gratified to see
that you are strong, healthy, bright,
lively, and inquisitive —
a real boy, who promises to provide
many interesting, provocative, and
challenging, as well as loving and memorable
moments, incidents, and experiences,
for your parents, sister, and you
during the years ahead.

Although I shall not be here to share and enjoy
those wondrous and exciting years,
I shall be with you in spirit,

cheering and supporting you on your journey
thought childhood, adolescence, and adulthood
— and reveling in the accomplishments and successes
I predict that your will experience
in the future.

I end this missive with a very old Irish prayer:
May the road rise up to meet you.
May the wind always be at your back.
May the sun shine warm upon your face,
and rains fall soft upon your fields.
And until we meet again,
May God hold you in the palm of His hand.

For my first great grandson
The last gift in a long life
one to be treasured
HAPPY BIRTHDAY!
Love,
Great Poppi

Haiku

If God sends you down
A steep and stony pathway
May you have strong shoes

May God's smile light you
Nearby neighbors respect you
And Angels greet you

For Dennis on His 61st Birthday

Another year has passed
on our individual life journeys.
But there are some important people and events
that we happily share.
Five persons illustrate the gemstone "people" facet:
First and foremost, your wife,
and my daughter, Kathleen;
second, your stepdaughter
and my granddaughter, Tamra,
and third, your step granddaughter
and my great granddaughter, Kaila;
fourth, your stepson and my grandson, Sean.
and fifth, his wife, my daughter-in-law, Leah.
I have watched with great pleasure,
satisfaction, and delight,
your admirable, yes, sterling and special relationships
and love for all of those people
with close and special family ties to me.
The events aspect
includes visits, holidays, wedding, christenings,
birthday parties, and other family get-togethers.
I am grateful that our relationships,
affiliations, and contacts
have invariably been cordial.
amicable, friendly, and affectionate.
I close this greeting with
the following desideration and prayers:
To my son-in-law, Dennis,
with the very best of wishes
for a very happy day,
one he will long remember
in a very pleasant way.

And the very best of wishes
for a year that's happy too,
filled with all the nicest things
selected especially for you,

My ardent prayers for you follow:
May you be blessed with good health,
happy, interesting, and new
by the love of Kathy, Kaila.
as well as by your family, relatives, and friends.
HAPPY BIRTHDAY!

Haiku

Enjoy "small" things now
The "big" things will come later
Face them at that time

In baseball parlance
A pitcher's best redeemer
A fast double play

That which is not checked
Often gets out of control
Avoid that mistake

For Grace on Her Seventh Birthday

What can a very old and far away
great grandfather say to his beautiful
and next-to-the-youngest Tracey descendant—
especially when he has not seen her in person
for more than five years.
First, he says, "I love you with all my heart."
And then he says, "I missed seeing you
grow from a beautiful baby into a lovely young girl."
And then he continues:
I also miss
The things you say and do,
Your smiles and laughter,
Your warmth and kindness,
Your charm and beauty,
The peace, hope, and joy you bring
to everyone around you.
You are a special gift,
not only to your Mom and Dad,
your brother David,
your grandparents, aunts and uncles,
and your many cousins,
but also to the oldest member
of your extended family,
your 91-year-old Grand Poppi!
In addition, Grace Marie you are
Smart as a whip
Pretty as a picture
Cute as a kitten
Busy as a bee
Curious as a puppy
Bright as a new penny

Warm as toast
Sweet as honey
Endearing as a ponytail
Captivating as dimples
Talkative as a magpie
Happy as a lark
So Gracie is all of the above—
and much more, too!
I have just run out of words
to describe all of her
beguiling attributes and characteristics.
So, she has to know and understand
why and how much she is loved
by her great grandfather
and everyone who has met her,
HAPPY BIRTHDAY!
Love,
Great Poppi

Haiku

Make healthy choices
Practice moderation now
To enjoy good health

The key to long life
Stay positive in outlook
Don't sweat the small stuff

Remember this truth
Happiness lies in the heart
Not in the venue

For Jackie L. on Her 59th Birthday

You are a special gift,
not only to your Mom and Dad,
your brothers Jay and Paul,
their spouses and their children,
your aunts and uncles, your cousins,
and your many friends and coworkers,
but also to the oldest member
of your extended family,
your loving godfather, Bill.

You're someone who brings happiness
to everyone you know.
The world becomes a better place
wherever you go.
You're like a ray of sunshine
that gives life a warmer touch,
and that is the special reason
you're admired and loved
by so many and so very much.
So, you will always be special,
you will always be loved
for the kindhearted way that you live.
And you will always be wished
joyful days in return
for the warmhearted happiness
that you never fail to give..

Here are my prayers for you on this auspicious day
and every day for the rest of your life:
Protection from the wind
A sturdy roof to keep out the rain

Steaming hot tea beside the fire
Laughter of friends to cheer you
And those you love near you
May you also have warm words on a cold evening
A full moon on a dark night,
the road downhill all the way to your door,
and everything else that your heart might desire!
HAPPY BIRTHDAY

Haiku

Living on the Cape
There's no other place like it
Excepting Heaven

A sure sign of spring
Mating tree frogs trilling
The peepers at work

Make healthy choices
Practice moderation now
To enjoy long life

The only thing worse
Than a severe thunderstorm
Is a bad workday

Remember this truth
Happiness lies in the heart
Not in the venue

On Steve's 56th Birthday

Although I know very few of the details about your trials
as a husband and father during the last few years,
I do know that life has given you challenges.
That situation, as I'm sure you're fully aware,
is the destiny of most of us, myself included.
Serious challenges occurred in my infancy,
childhood, and especially in my 'teen years'.
With the grace of God, and the help of my
Aunt Josephine (who later became my foster mother),
my sainted wife, Kathleen, and six wonderful children,
I not only survived, but also matured and prospered.
In addition, my saving grace was my refusal
to be defined by troubles and adverse events.
I believe that your current situation,
although not what you and Maura want most,
can become what you need, given enough time.
So, I am impressed by your attitude toward life
in both the present and the future.
I just want you to know that I not only admire
and respect you as a man and a would-be husband,
legally my son-in-law, and also my friend.
You should also know the truth about me:
I rarely make my feelings known to others.
This piece of verse is an exception
to one of my rules of conduct —
because I probably will have very few opportunities
to tell people close to me, including my children
and grandchildren, how deeply I appreciate and love them.
So time is now of the essence!
I must take advantage of the time that is left to do so.
Here is what I have learned about Stephen Mottley:
You are blessed with the God-given

talent of making every minute of every day count,
by finding adventure, enjoyment,
and excitement in the little, even trivial things.
Some people just wake up, get up, go to work,
do their job, return home —
and repeat that ritualistic pattern the next day
and the day after, and for months and years on end.
But you have that rare ability and inclination
to give even the smallest moments
and mundane, everyday events genuine meaning—
and communicate that significant message to others.
You are also a master listener —
a person who not only hears the words being voiced
but also comprehends the intent of the speaker.
and internalizes the meaning of the communication.
HAPPY BIRTHDAY!

A Belated Birthday Retrospective

You have my sincere apology
for my failure to remember your natal day.
Let me now extend my overdue
but loving congratulations
and sincere best wises on your birthday.
My ardent prayers for you follow:
May you be blessed with good health,
happy, interesting, and rewarding years, soon to be
enhanced and totally encircled by the love of a child
as well as by your family, relatives. and friends.
I also ask for multiple opportunities for you
to use the God-given talents, abilities, and capacities
that will enable you to be happy and productive.
May the Year 2015 bring you good fortune,
good health, and every joy.

My Goddaughter, Christine Anne

My sister-in-law Terri (Mannix) O'Neill,
my brother Jim's wife,
gave me the honor of choosing her only child's given name
as Christine or Deirdre (the legendary heroine of Ireland}.
As brother Jim's best man and godfather-to-be,
I chose the name of one of our O'Neill favorite aunts,
our Dad's sister, Christine.
Christine has dual citizenship in the US and Portugal.
She was born in Boston,
christened in West Roxbury, attended grammar
and high school in West Roxbury,
and graduated from Wellesley College,
in the town of Wellesley, just West of Boston.
The college, one of the original Seven Sisters Colleges,
consistently ranks among the top 10 liberal arts colleges
in the United States.

Christine married Paulo António deSousa e Sá,
an officer in the Portuguese Navy. while he was a student
at the Massachusetts Institute of Technology in Cambridge
A graduate of the Portuguese Naval Academy,
Portuguese Naval War College, and MIT's
School of Naval Architecture until he retired years later.
Christine and Palo have two daughters, Sarah and Carolina

Christine and Paulo have reared Sara and Carolina, two talent
and accomplished daughters —
in terms of education and prestigious professional positions
They're very proud of them, as they should be.
Sarah is 29+ now, 7+ years out of University of Edinburgh
(MA in Social Anthropology & Sociology)

and a Master of International Relations,
summa cum laude, Catholic University of Lisbon.
Recently, Sarah married her partner of 3 years,
João, a fellow anthropologist.
They live in the Alfama, the ancient neighborhood
on the hill right below St. George's castle.

Carolina now 18+, is in her senior year at St Julian's
finishing the International Baccalaureate diploma.
An excellent all-around athlete, she plays soccer,
as well as varsity basketball and volleyball.
She has applied to five universities in the UK,
and visited two of them, Exeter and Oxford Brookes.
She prefers Oxford Brookes for its dynamism,
international student body, and its location in Oxford,
a short distance from the ancient colleges.
Although more exuberant and outgoing than her sister,
Carolina is an equally excellent student,
very well adjusted, and enjoys an active social life.
She is extremely responsible about her studies
and sensible in her attitude toward life.
Christine and Paulo have been truly blessed with their girls,
and they give them great happiness.

Unfortunately, there is a years-long gap in my
direct personal contacts with Jim, Terri, and Sarah-
and have never had even one meeting with Carolina.
The hiatus began shortly after Jim and Terri were married
and continued without contacts until I retired from
from my civilian job at Fort Devens — except for one visit
when I arrived in Naval uniform uninvited at their home
one Sunday evening — after completing my weekend duty
at the Naval Air Station in South Weymouth.

I often wondered why I saw Jim and Terri so infrequently,
and even drew some conclusions about its cause.
Nonetheless, I still have no real answers.
The matter is undoubtedly better left alone.
Whatever the source, it was completely forgotten
during the last few years of Jim and Terri's lives.
We enjoyed our frequent meetings at 14 Vermont Street.
I remember clearly our visit to Portugal June 17-26. 1992
It was a great adventure for Terri and me
and was memorialized in our book,
Journey to the Garden of Europe.

During Jim and Terri's last few years,
We met about every two or three weeks,
when I often brought my homemade soup and sandwiches
or took Jim out to a local pub for lunch.
On those visits, I read sections of *The Indomitable O'Neill*
(that I was transcribing and editing from tapes).
I had to make certain that I interpreted his words correctly
and make a final check of the accuracy of my efforts.
It was a very difficult task because Jim had suffered
a stroke earlier and was working to regain
his vocabulary and speech fluency.
It was well worth the effort,
and both of us were proud of the final product.

About two years ago, Christine and Paulo moved from
Carcavelos to the next town, Parede,
in a house with a back garden, and a lovely view of the sea
I wish that I could visit them, but that cannot happen.

Bill Jr.'s 67th Birthday

So, now I have a newly minted "Down Easter,"
formerly given the much less complimentary
nom de plume of Maineac.
I guess that is appropriate, even more apt
than a state that advocates, "Live Free or Die!"
I trust that you and Suzanne are well and happy—
and have now thawed out
from a long and truly Arctic winter.
I don't know whether you are now old enough
to require indoor temperatures above 70 degrees —
but at 91, I most certainly do —74 or 75!
I hope and pray that you have not relapsed to the
life style and bad habit of something
over a year ago —or is it now two years ago?
As I warned you at that time, a return to your former habit
would surely kill you—and leave your three children
badly in need of a caring father.
Their attitudes and behavior in the last few years,
including their lack of contact with their grandfather,
indicates that they need your help and guidance now.
I am also disappointed that it has now been
nine months since I last saw you.
I realize that you have been busy
and that the distance from Maine to Cape Cod
is an impediment rather than a mere inconvenience,
but I don't see any of my sons (or their children) very often,
and my time on earth is quickly running out.
I realize that this missive, meant to be a happy birthday wish,
sounds more like a series or catenation of complaints.
Despite that, I do wish for you and your family
the very best that life has to offer this coming year
and the many years that will follow.

For Siara on Her 13th Birthday

Today you are a teenager —
with all the perquisites and benefits that herald
or formally proclaim your new status as a young adult.
Of course there are also some negatives
associated with the 'teen years
as advertised by the use of such cynical terms
as teenybopper, teener, juvenile, and adolescent.
But your grandfather sees you as a vibrant,
stunning talented, accomplished,
and brilliant young woman,
one with an extraordinary and dazzling future.
You have all of the attributes, skills, and personality
of a winner, a world champion
in whatever career you choose to pursue.
You could become a renowned vocalist,
win The Antoinette Perry Stage Acting Award,
an Academy Award for "best" or "supporting" actress,
or a TV Emmy Award.
Or you could easily become
a noted writer, editor, or novelist —
or a "somebody" in an entirely different profession.
So, set your goals high.
Don't sell yourself short! Work hard!
Be all that you can be!
Know, too, that your Tracey grandfather will be watching
and applauding you from "the other side"
with great enthusiasm, pride, and love.

Haiku
The past is prelude
To the rest of one's future
Ignore and regret.

A Father's Roles

If you've ever heard the threat,
"Wait until your father comes home,"
you probably grew up in a family where,
if you had done something wrong,
you feared the moment
your dad walked in the door,
home from his day's work.
Dads are often viewed
as the "go-to" parent for discipline,
sound advice, and playtime partner,
while mothers are the "go-to" parent
for sympathy, nurturing, and comfort.
But, fathers matter more than
just serving as the person in the family
who is expected to rule with an iron fist..

A daughter may outgrow your lap,
but she can never outgrow your heart.
Your daughter may be a beautiful girl
but, even if she is not pretty,
her father holds her tiny hand walks with her
like she's a lovely little angel.
He is giving her the greatest gifts a girl
can get: self-confidence, protection, and love.
And a little girl learns to honor and trust the man in her life,
and the things that the world expects from women:
to be beautiful, to soothe troubled psyches,
bring gifts or send greeting cards, make the cookies —
all of those things become the way
daughters usually pay fathers back
for loving and protecting them.

The "Trials" of Lin Li Tracey.
While Earning Her Juris Doctor Degree

Deciding which of the many
prestigious and available law schools
to apply for admission,
including the top-rated Ivy League Harvard Law School,
but ruling it out for many reasons, including costs.
Selecting the University of New Hampshire School of Law
as a viable choice due to its proximity and a scholarship offe
Accepting admission to the fall class in 2013,
thereby assuming the rigors of an intensive academic challeng
Securing the enthusiastic endorsement, encouragement,
commitment, and support of husband, Kevin.
Deferring her choice of ultimate practice of law,
such as, banking, commercial, corporate, consumer, contract
criminal, employment, family, health, immigration, insuranc
labor, personal injury, tax, tort, or a wide range
of other areas of law until later in her academic career.
Embarking on her new regimen and demanding schedule,
consisting mainly of intensive library and home study,
class and seminar attendance,
with little or no time left for sleep or recreation.
Dealing with such esoteric subjects as
Foundations of Law, Civil Procedures,
Constitutional Law, Contracts, Criminal Law,
Legal Analysis, Property, and Torts —
and an entirely new and required mastery
of Latin words and phrases—
including *a priori* and *a posteriori*.
ad hominen and *animus nocendi*,
corpus delecti and *corpus juris*,
de facto and *de jure*, *ex cathedra* and *ex gratia*,

guardian ad litem, habeus corpus, and *in extremis,*
in flagrante delicto and *in loco parentis,*
bona fide and *male fide, nolo contendere,* and *non compos*
mentos, noto bene and *persona non grata,*
pro bono, post mortem, and *prima facie,*
o tempore and *quid pro quo,* and *sui juris* and *vinculum juris.*
And sooner or later she must learn about famous attorneys,
such a as Johnny Cochrane, Alan Dershowitz,
Robert Shapiro, F. Lee Bailey, Shawn Holley Chapman,
and Anne Bremner.
And let us not overlook some famous and infamous laws,
Roe v. Wade (decriminalized abortion),
Civil Rights Acts, Voting Rights Act.
and Affordable Health Care Act (Obamacare).
So, with my best wishes for a rewarding
And challenging academic experience
and a fascinating and monetarily satisfying career,
I send my love and a HAPPY BIRTHDAY
to my youngest and newest daughter-in-law.

Haiku

A good dad is worth
More than one hundred teachers
In a youngster's life

An essential truth
Once I was my daddy's son
Now I'm my son's dad.

For Tamra on Her 39th Birthday

Your birthday is a special day—
one that's just for you —.
a time for doing everything
that you truly like to do.
And on this day
that belongs only to you,
the wish this verse brings
is for the joy you so deserve
and all life's nicest things.
Because you're someone special,
this verse comes to wish you:
A wonderful birthday —
shared with those you love—
Kaila, Jimmy, and Dennis,
your sister-in–law, Leah,
and your brother, Sean,
And first among those you love,
your life-long supporter,
your exceptional mother, Kathy,
who has always been,
and will always be there for you.
My feelings for you are always
warm in my heart.
And I need to let you know
how much you mean to me.
You're really someone special
for everything you are to me.
I have many memories
of happy times we've shared,
of moments full of love
wherever and whenever
we've been together.

Thank you for being your wonderful self—
someone I have always
and will always love.
Wishing you the kind of day
You truly deserve—
A day that leaves you feeling loved—
because that's exactly what you are!
Happy Birthday!

Failings and Fallibility

Life should never be a game of one-upmanship,
personal attacks, or "got-chas."
We must recognize the futility of "losing it" —
temper tantrums, retribution, punishment,
or other forms of payback —
and holding a grudge is also unacceptable.
. Whenever someone does something wrong or hurtful,
his or her apology must be graciously accepted
and the transgressor forgiven.
Other responses are also inappropriate —
and often damaging, even irreparable.
In some families, cutoffs,
or silent treatments are *pro forma*
and may last months, even years.
To be vindictive is the greatest sin of all.
We all must recognize the fallibility of humans.
We must, as a family, love each other
regardless of mistakes or lapses in self-control.
The unforgiving game is a "no no,"
as are hurtful, insensitive, cruel,
or offensive words or actions.
Love and forgiveness conquer all.

For Kaylyn on Her 14th Birthday

My, how quickly the years fly by!
You are my sixth granddaughter,
of the total of 12 grandchildren,
who has reached the second year
of her 'teens.
Although that is not particularly
unusual or remarkable,
it is certainly very noteworthy.
What is special, even extraordinary.
is the lovely and talented little lady
you have become in the last several years!
Although I have not been able to see you
as often or as long
as I would like to be with you,
my age-related limitations and restrictions
on my travel and other activities—
as well as your very hectic
and demanding school and artistic schedules —
make that simply unworkable.
However, that fact does not mean
that I don't think about you everyday —
and every night, too, in my bedtime prayers.
I love my Kaylyn very much,
and I want the very best things in life for her,
both now and in the future!
As you can see, I am trying with little success
to find the perfect words
to tell you how much you're loved—
but words that powerful and inspired
are all too few.

When a granddaughter as stunning
and cherished as you are,
all there is to say again …
I love you!
You are a wonderful gift,
and my life is richer and better
because you're in it.

For Lina on Her 45th Birthday

Here are some of the clichés that fit Lina,
one of my four daughters-in-law
Lina is as:
Smart as a fox and quick as a cat.
Bright as a new penny and pretty as a doll.
Cute as a kitten and lovely as a daisy.
Busy as a beaver and curious as a puppy.
Warm as the autumn light and sweet as a sugarplum.
Winsome as a close friend and charming as a princess.
Endearing as a forehead kiss and intriguing as an accent.
Captivating as dimples and engaging as an Irish seanchaí.
Independent as a tigress and stubborn when she's right.
Talkative as a parakeet and happy as a lark.
Feminine as a woman should be.
Loving as only a mother can be.
So Lina is all of the above—
and much more, too!
I have just run out of words
to describe all of her
beguiling attributes and persona.
So, she has to know and understand
why and how much she is admired and loved
by everyone, including her father-in-law.
HAPPY BIRTHDAY!

For Kolby on Her 15th Birthday

As a young woman whose birth occurred
on the Eve of the day before Christ was born,
you're a perfect reflection of God's love.
You are one of those extraordinary people
who keeps the spirit of Christmas
shining brightly throughout the year.
For that you are truly loved!

The things you say and do
Your smiles and laughter,
Your warmth and kindness,
Your charm and beauty,
Bring peace, hope, and joy
To everyone around you.
For that you are truly loved!

God has blessed me by giving you to me
as a loving granddaughter.
I pray every night that He will bless you
with everything that you need,
everything that is truly good,
and that His love will always light your way.
For that you are truly loved!

Because your life is a true reflection of God's love
These are my prayers and wishes for you:
That your Christmas day be perfect,
That the day be precious and faultless,
That the New Year be ideal, too,
And that this day and the month and years ahead
Will be very bright and exactly right for you.
Remember that your Poppi
Loves you and always will.

For Kaila on Her 8th Birthday

Here are some of the clichés that fit Kaila,
one of my eight granddaughters
and one of my two great granddaughters,
Kaila Lee is:
Smart as a whip and quick as a cat.
Bright as a button and pretty as a picture.
Cute as a kitten and lovely as a summer day.
Busy as a bee and loving as a little mother.
Curious as a puppy and bright as a new penny.
Warm as toast ad sweet as honey.
Winsome as a sparrow and charming as a princess.
Endearing as ponytails.
Intriguing as a tattoo and captivating as dimples.
Engaging as texting and independent as a lioness.
Stubborn as a mule and talkative as a magpie.
Happy as a lark and feminine as a girl can be.
So Kaila is all of the above—
and much more, too!
I have just run out of words
to describe all of her
beguiling attributes and characteristics.
So, she has to know and understand
why and how much she is loved
by her great grandfather
HAPPY BIRTHDAY!

For Siara on Her 12th Birthday

Only 12 months remain before you become a teenager!
That is the onset of womanhood by many standards —
physical, social, and emotional.
The change in my stunning granddaughter
over the last two years has been phenomenal!
From a lovely but very reserved youngster,
you have transformed yourself into a warm, outgoing,
highly communicative, and lovely young woman —
as well as a very talented actress and vocalist.
You have my compliments and deep personal pride
in your outstanding musical and other accomplishments
at the recent Massachusetts Jazz Educators
High School Competition.
At that event you distinguished yourself
as an extraordinarily gifted
and accomplished performer,
as well as a lovely and charming young lady.
You are also blessed with an engaging personality,
one that augments your dazzling talents.
Thoughts of you and prayerful best wishes
are never far from my mind.
So, Siara, I pray every night
that God will bless you every day that lies ahead.
I also ask that God fill your birthday
and the years that follow
with happiness, the gift of good health,
and that the joy you have brought to others,
Blossom for you today and every day of your life.
HAPPY BIRTHDAY!

For Mikie on Her 34th Birthday

Although I have not seen you very often
in the years you have been 3,000 miles away,
please know that you are often in my thoughts
and in my prayers every night.
I missed watching you grow from childhood,
and through adolescence, to become
the beautiful and talented woman that you are.
Although I regret that loss of direct contact,
it is how life sometimes works,
but it has had no diminishing or withering
effect on caring and love.
I have noted with great pride
that you completed college
and have been eminently successful managing
Ride the Ducks of Seattle.
It is equally satisfying to know that your Dad
gives you plaudits and credit for your
contributions to the growth and development
of that highly successful business.
Remember always that I love you
and that I will always
be here for you, at least in spirit,
as you live and prosper
in terms of love given and returned,
as well as in the realm of material things.
My wish for you on this special day:
May the joy you have brought to others
bloom for you today and every day henceforth,
that you have now found
the true love of your life, and that you will soon find
a solution to the travel dilemma you both face.

On Laine and Ben's Wedding Day

Today is the second most important day of your lives.
The day of your birth was the first.
You don't even remember that historic event.
However, you'll always remember this day — Guaranteed!
It marks the beginning of your new life,
a life you fully share for the first time
with any other human being.
For today, you have given each other the greatest gift
that anyone can give to another —
total love and commitment of mind, body, and soul.
Your family, relatives, and friends rejoice with you
on this auspicious day and wish for you henceforth,
every blessing that God and your loved ones can bestow —
among them, long and productive lives,
fitness and vitality, joy and happiness,
and everything else that will be useful to you in God's plan
And here is another heartfelt wish for you.
My hope and prayers are that you will have children —
loving, healthy, and happy children —
if that is God's plan and your wish,
because that, in my own experience,
is the greatest gift of all.
God love you both, this day and always.
Full of warm moments to remember
to last the coming years through.
Wishing you the kind of years you deserve—
ones that leave you feeling loved—
because that's just exactly what you are!
Poppi
09 /28//2013

A Prayer for Laine and Ben

rd, God of Hope, look with favor upon our children, Laine
d Ben, who have pledged their love for each other by
changing their vows of fidelity. Grant this young woman and
s young man the blessings you have given to parents, their
andparents, and us in such abundance.

rd, God of Love, we pray that Laine and Ben's love for each
er, so bright and shining today, may never tarnish. Rather,
it increase in depth and luster as they share and grow in
derstanding of each other's needs.

rd, bless Laine and Ben with healthy, happy, and loving chil-
en as we, their parents and grandparents, have been blessed.
ant them health and long lives of devotion to each other, their
nilies, and their friends.

rd, help Laine and Ben pursue their chosen vocations with
ill and understanding, whether it be with the expertise of a
rporate training and development professional, the tender
uch of a wife and mother, the skills of a federal government
nefits administrator, or the devotion of a loving husband and
her. Let them exemplify in their lives the standards and
lues You have taught.

rd, God of peace, grant Laine and Ben the blessing of living
ir lifetimes in a peaceful world. And, if adversity is destined
be a part of their future, grant them the strength to face their
als with courage and composure.

d finally, Lord, grant Laine and Ben the grace to grow in
derstanding of Your wishes and help them to remain faithful
Your commands. We ask in the name of your Son. Amen.

For Jackie M. on Her 37th Birthday

I don't believe that my children or grandchildren
know what is most important to me
and has always held first place in my heart and life.
It is my family.
And the reasons for its significance
relate to its size as well as to its dispersion.
The O'Neill-Burgoyne, Doheny-Ahola family is large:
8, 14, 7, and 4 in our parents' generation, the grandchildren
of Thomas O'Neill and Anne Dunne; Nelson Burgoyne
and Minnie Trudell; John Doheny and Hannah Flynn;
and Kalle Ahola and Ida Siipola, total 74 children.
As you know, your Nanni's and my marriage added six,
followed by their 14 spouses or companions,
12 children and their
4 spouses, and 3 great grandchildren.
The total number of close relatives now exceeds 160
The family is now represented by a great variety
of nationalities and cultures:
Irish, French, Finnish, French Canadian, Native American,
Jewish, Chinese, African American, Swiss,
and Latino-Hispanics.
Those relatives now live in the Northwest (Washington State
New England, Maine, New Hampshire, Vermont, Connecticu
Massachusetts, and Portugal
as well as in Northern New York, New Jersey and Florida.
Regrettably, your children are unlikely to see many
of their first cousins
and other relatives that follow, due to future marriages
and births of children.
Unfortunately, the family will develop more strangers,
but there is nothing that can be done about that.
I anticipated that when your family moved to Washington.

ave traveled out there only four times, twice with your Nanni
and twice more for your and Mikie's weddings.
Although I have seen Grace once here on Cape,
I have yet to meet David (lately remedied!),
I hope that will happen, but the likelihood
of my ever seeing him is growing smaller and
smaller as my health deteriorates and my remaining
time on earth becomes shorter.
nyway, you have hundreds of close relatives scattered over a
y large area. Unfortunately, you will not meet many of them.
HAPPY BIRTHDAY!

Remembering

There's a special sort of feeling
when you talk about our family.
It's a pleasure to remember
all the happy times we've had.
There's a special kind of caring
that's meant for them alone
There's a special place somewhere
within our hearts only they can own.
There's a special sort of feeling
that's warm and loving too.
A special kind of pride that comes
with every thought of all of you.
I have so many memories
of happy times we've shared,
of moments full of love whenever
we've been together.
Thank you for those moments…
And thank you for being
my wonderful family—
people I will always love.

For Victor on His 15th Birthday

You are now approaching your mid-teens.
I remember those years very clearly.
I was a sophomore at Leominster High School,
and life was not very smooth for me.
During those years, my foster father, Edward,
was constantly on my case, telling me
that I was good for nothing, lazy and stupid,
and would never amount to anything —
although I was quite useful in days off from school,
serving as his unpaid plumber's helper!
However, I survived those difficult years
and learned some critical lessons from that experience.
I am happy to have observed, and now note with much pride
that you have already learned
the most important of those maxims:

Believe in yourself and your capabilities.
Those in positions to judge you, even teachers,
will often be wrong.

You must have been told and know with certainty
that the world is a better place
because you are here.

And here are some more mundane axioms.
although they, too, are very important:

Always return phone calls
and reply to letters as soon as possible

Always be on time for appointments and meetings —
be there at least five minutes early.

Always acknowledge correspondence and gifts
within 5 days of receipt.

Always honor your commitments
and keep your promises

Always double check written communications
before mailing them or hitting the send button.

Always prepare thoroughly for participating
in conferences, panels, interviews, and symposia
— and carefully rehearse oral presentations.

Always be in control of your emotions
and their pronouncement
by body language, words, and facial expressions.

Always remember that you can't get things done
if you stay in a rut or on a racetrack.

To Whom Much is Given (and You are in that Category),
Much More is Expected in Return

And always remember that ego is the anesthetic
that God has given to man to deaden the pain
of being a damn fool.

May all your hopes and dreams come true
HAPPY BIRTHDAY!
Love,
Poppi/Abuelo

For Kathy B. on Her 62nd Birthday

I must have said this before,
but it's worth repeating:
Your birthday is a very special day.
It is one that I remember so very clearly
even after 62 years!
This day is one that is just for you.
It's a time for doing anything and everything
you honestly and enthusiastically love to do.
So, on this day that belongs only to you,
the wish this verse brings
is for the joy and comfort you so deserve,
as well as all life's nicest things.
I know that life has not always been
a bed of roses for you.
But, troubles and difficult times
are the fates of most of us and are not unusual.
Fortunately, the good and happy times
invariably outnumber the trying times.
So, as an Irish proverb asserts and insists:
Remember always to forget
the troubles that have passed away....
But remember to remember
the benefits, gifts, and blessings of every day.
Keep in mind, too, your happy heritage:
you are the mirror image of your sainted mother,
bear the identical first and middle names,
share her professional degree and teaching skills,
and most important of all, her love of children—
not just her own, but all children.

And last, remember this too:
You are one of two daughters who
have made my life better on a regular rather than
on a "sometimes" schedule.
Because of both of you,
I know what real closeness means.
And that's about as blessed as anyone can get.
HAPPY BIRTHDAY!

Mental Health Haiku

Three hundred fifty
The number of disorders
In the DSM

An analog man
In today's digital world
A bad place to be

The new abnormal
Addiction: the Internet
Binge eating disease

Never seek the truth
Simply avoid opinions
On any subject

It's far easier
To forgive an enemy
Than getting even

For Leah on Her 38ᵗʰ Birthday

This free verse is written for someone very special.
On this auspicious and propitious day
thirty-eight years ago,
God blessed the Brandon family
by giving them a beautiful baby girl,
one who was destined
to become my grandson Sean's wife
and my granddaughter-in-law.
I pray every night that He will bless you and Sean
with everything that you need,
everything that is truly good,
in the months and years ahead.
And I also pray that His love
will always guide your way.
For the gifts with which you have been blessed
you are truly admired and loved!
For you and Sean are two of those rare people
who exemplify and keep the true spirit of family
glowing brightly and steadfastly
throughout the year.
For you are authentic reflections of God's love.
Know that you are truly loved by the Tracey family
for the following gifts and talents:
The things you say and do
Your smiles and laughter,
Your warmth and kindness,
Your charm and beauty,
The peace, hope, and joy you
display and offer
to everyone around you.
For those gifts you are truly loved!

Let me close this missive
by repeating an old sailor's plea and prayer for his
granddaughter-in-law
May you have blue skies and calm following seas o
for the rest of your life.
HAPPY BIRTHDAY!

More Irish Blessings

Wherever you go
and whatever you do,
May the luck of the Irish
be there with you.

May your neighbors respect you
Trouble neglect you,
The angels protect you
And Heaven accept you
And the light of God shine on you

With the very best of wishes
For a very happy day,
One you'll long remember
In a very pleasant way
And the very best of wishes
For a year that's happy too,
Filled with all the nicest things
selected especially for you

May you have the gift of FAITH.
The blessing of HOPE
And the peace of His LOVE
On your birthday,
This year and always.

For Jackie L's Birthday

What follow are the mental meanderings
of your nonagenarian godfather —
although a very old man, one blessed
with a very good long-term memory
His reminiscences of you
over a period of more than 57 years
reveal some significant gaps
in the whole story of your life.
Although there are many key reasons
for those blank spaces in my memories
of my first goddaughter,
there are many other events worthy of commentary.
Although I admit that I don't clearly recall
your baptism in 1955,
when Kathleen and I became your godparents,
I don't remember the name of the church
or even the town in which the sacrament was celebrated
(although I believe that it was Westboro).
I do remember the priest's white alb and stole,
the baptismal font, the holy water poured on your head
the anointing with holy oils, the promises Kay and I made,
and other essentials of the Sacrament of Baptism,
as the priest and godparents performed their functions.
I also remember that Kay and I visited you
and your parents quite often in Westboro,
in the ranch-style house close to the railroad tracks.
I also remember clearly the many summer visits
we made to the original dwelling
at Surfside Drive in West Dennis
when you were a charming young girl
— and later a lovely teenager.

And, a few years later, I was delighted and impressed
with your choice of nursing as your profession.
I also clearly remember your garden wedding
and the reception, dinner,
and dancing to Scott's band indoor.
I'm sure that you don't know that I was tempted
to sing my favorite song, *Pennies from Heaven*,
for you and Scott, but mercifully for all present,
I managed to resist that impulse.
I confess that I was unable to control that inclination
at my 90th birthday party when I succumbed
to the entreaties of my children and grandchildren
to sing my favorite song one more time.
But, here is the one thing I truly want you to know:
I have remembered you by name for many years
in my nightly prayers, asking the Lord and Kathleen
to watch over and protect you from all harm.
I conclude this missive with these wishes:
May everything wondrous and everything bright
be yours on your birthday from morning 'till night.
And then through the coming years,
may the same wonders hold true,
so that every day is filled with life's best gifts for you!
Happy Birthday!

Haiku

Be open and bold
Let your persona shine through
You'll be in demand

Live your greatest dreams
If not turned to advantage
They're gone forever

For Steve on Birthday LV

Many people have often told me,
including family, friends, and strangers,
that I really look "great" or "good."
My retort has invariably been.
Thanks, but I wish that I felt as well as I look.
I also realize that as soon as one turns 90,
people, young and old, treat you differently.
When people say that you look good,
they don't mean that you look handsome,
they just mean that you're alive.
It's simply a way of letting you know
that you give them hope that they may live
as long as you have lived.
You too, can count your blessings.
Although you have lived only 11/18th (61.1 percent)
of the years I have reached,
you remain in good health and physical shape
and your mental acuity and powers remain robust.
So, if you continue with your well-balanced diet
and regular fitness and exercise routine,
you should easily match or exceed my record of longevity.
To achieve that goal,
as well as continue feeling alive and relevant,
I also highly recommend that you
surround yourself with young people
as often and as much as possible.
Your son and daughter can provide much of that contact,
and Laine and Ben can also
contribute to the fulfillment of that need.
Although there are limits to what that will do,
the company of young men and women will certainly help.

Of course, despite her chronological age,
Maura will always be a wellspring
of youthful perspectives and activities
for both of you.
I close with this Irish blessing:
May your mornings bring joy,
And your evenings bring peace.
May your troubles grow few
And your blessings increase.
Sincerely and cordially,
HAPPY BIRTHDAY!

Haiku

A good dad is worth
More than one hundred teachers
In a youngster's life

An essential truth
Once I was my daddy's son
Now I'm my son's dad.

An important fact:
A son first frustrates his dad
Six months before birth.

As a boy I did
What my father demanded
When is it my turn?

For Lina on Her Birthday

Another year has quickly vanished
for you as well as for me.
However, there is a very important difference
between the early forties and nineties.
Planning for the future is an exercise in futility for me.
Planning for the years ahead is indispensable for you!

I hope your birthday dreams and wishes
Will combine with all the rest
To fill your special day with happiness
And make it truly the best.

May your days be filled with joy
From morning 'till night
Each and every day filled with sunshine
And things for you to take delight!

May God bless you in the morning
With His presence shining bright
To make your whole day happy
With His radiant love and light.

May God bless you in the evening
When the daytime hours depart.
And like a blessing or special benediction,
Leave His peace within your heart.

HAPPY BIRTHDAY!

For Laine on Her 28th

This is the year that you and Ben will be wed
Saturday, September 8th, I believe.
I hope that I will be able to make it,
but I can't guarantee that.
However, I can assure you that
wherever I am, still living on Cape Cod,
or on the other side at the BNC
next to your Nanni,
I'll be observing
that momentous celebration.
Ben is a good man and, in my opinion,
a first-rate choice.
I also promise that you both
will continue to be in my nightly prayers.
when I pray for long, healthy,
and happy lives for you,
with rewarding jobs, loyal friends,
and healthy and happy children,
if that is both yours
and God's will.
Those precious gifts are never issued,
they must always be earned
by unconditional love,
unremitting understanding,
unrelenting patience,
assiduous persistence
unvarying tolerance,
and unyielding devotion.
God bless you
HAPPY BIRTHDAY!

For My Grandson on His 26th Birthday

Because you have again failed
to acknowledge receipt
of the verse I sent you last year.
I repeat the message here.
I do not understand your
reluctance (or refusal)
to respond or even to thank me
for the ID jewelry I sent to you recently.
This will be my final attempt
to contact the only grandson to carry my name.
My disappointment, regret, and frustration
are unbearable and unwarranted.
What a shame!
*****

You probably didn't notice
that I did not compose a verse
nor send you a small check
for your last birthday.
However, that was not due
to the failing memory of your
octogenarian grandfather.
Rather it was a penalty
for your failure to acknowledge
those mementoes on your 23rd birthday,
and your repeated the blunder last Christmas.
As I have reminded you and your siblings,
I expend a considerable amount
of thought, time, energy, and love
writing those verses.
A short, hand-written note
E-mail, or phone call
of thanks is not only proper

but also an obligation of the recipient
of such gifts.
I did not have the heart
to deny you and your siblings
gifts for the last two Christmases —
despite the lack of thank you notes —
since all of you have received small gifts from me
every birthday and Christmas
since you were born.
In the future, I shall not
make the same mistake.
So, this will be the last of my gifts
on the occasions of your birthdays
and Christmases.
I leave this epistle with deep regret,
my heart-felt prayers, best wishes.
and this Irish Blessing:
May God be with you and Bless you.
May you be poor in misfortunes
and rich in blessings.
May you know nothing but happiness
from this day forward.
HAPPY BIRTHDAY

Haiku

Three essential traits
For success in any field
Smarts, grace, and wisdom

For My Godson, William R. Camiré

Precocious from birth and thriving thereafter!
Blessed with innumerable and formidable talents
and an insatiable appetite
for answers to such questions as,
What makes it work? Why does it do that?
That's Bill
In earlier years, an accomplished musician
with a God-given sense of true pitch.
Notably prodigious in terms of musicianship
on the guitar.
An accomplished kayaker with a love of the sport
and a healthy respect for rough water.
That's Bill
Never profane or blasphemous.
Under no circumstances irreverent or impious.
Typically predictable and invariably dependable.
Relentlessly thoughtful and unfailingly authentic.
Prudent and serious, but accessible and open.
An aficionado of food and drink
and an accomplished cook.
That's Bill
In other domains, he is a genuinely creative
and gifted genius,
a member of a distinctively unique genre
of creative people,
and again with a prodigious repertoire of skills.
He is a master photographer with an eye for composition
You name it, and he can shoot it well
That's Bill
Here is the other side of Bill:
A man for whom his Mom, Dad, and Siblings,

Andy, Paul, Tommy, and Bob,
have always been proud.
But, to all who really know, respect, and love him,
he is more than a talented and determined man.
Bill is a much-loved Son, Brother, Uncle, and Friend —
one who is always supportive and helpful
to all with whom he comes in contact.
After God made Bill, He destroyed the mold.

Haiku

Your first male godchild
A great gift in a man's life
One to be treasured

The future is now
Always make the right choices
Ask the right questions

Wear a "driving cap"
Tour with the "roof" wide open
In an MGB

Listen to these words
They are the songs of my life
Store them in your heart.

The oldest golfer
Wins the local golf tourney
Now that's newsworthy-

The O'Neill Irish Heritage

My Dad, James Edward O'Neill,
was conceived in Monasterevan, Ireland
and born, September 26, 1888 in Boston, MA,
just after immigrating to Boston.
His parents were Thomas Henry O'Neill
and Annie F. Dunne, both born in Ireland.
Dad was a proud Irishman
who enlisted in the US Navy October 11,1905
and served aboard the battleship USS
Rhode Island as it made its voyage around the world,
as a part of Theodore Roosevelt's Great White Fleet.
My Dad was honorably discharged
in the grade of Electrician's Mate 2nd Class,
October 10, 1908.
My grandfather, Thomas, was a skilled boot maker
(not a cobbler)
who trained my Dad to follow in his trade.
He then worked until the Great Depression
in the early 30s as a Prudential Insurance Company agent,
when he returned to his trade as a boot maker in Brookline
In the early 40s he returned to Leominster
and was hired by Fort Devens to design and fabricate
prostheses for soldiers with foot and toe malformations,
wounds, injuries, or accidents.
However, Dad never forgot that he and his family
are the sons and daughters of Ireland,
proud heirs of an ancient legacy.
The Irish have settled every corner of the globe,
driven from their homeland by famine and oppression,
or simply by the restless spirit that is our birthright.

herever the Irish have gone, they brought a love of freedom,
a droll humor, and a silver tongue.
Regardless of where destiny may take the Irish
they are linked to the land of their ancestral land
by a thread that reminds them always that
we are a unique people.
The Irish have made contributions
to world culture out of all proportion to their numbers.
), we Irish have every right to be proud of our Irish heritage.
Today, there are more people of Irish ancestry
living outside Ireland than within its borders.
I have one important regret: my younger brother,
John Joseph O'Neill
ever forgave me for allowing my name to be changed from
William Raymond O'Neill to
William Raymond Tracey,
when Edward P. and Josephine M. Tracey adopted me
in early 1940, just before high school graduation,
felt obliged to honor my foster parents for the many yeas of
nurturing, upbringing, and love they invested
in me for almost 18 years.
wed them much more than a name change, even though that
resulted in an apparent denial of my O'Neill heritage.

Haiku

The past is prelude
To the rest of one's future
Ignore and regret.

Don't live with regrets
Fix the emotive damage
By self-forgiveness

For Else-Marie on Valentine's Day

This poem uses the ***Words of Love***,
the actual titles of love songs
composed by songwriters
over many years, including 2012.
Those titles appear in bold italics
in the verses that follow.

When my wife of 53 years passed on,
I was completely devastated.
Then Came You.
That was the time
When I Fell in Love
It was at dinner
on a summer day at Polcari's,
a real ***Some Enchanted Evening***.

At Last, after waiting four long years,
I had ***Someone to Watch Over Me..***
You were the right one for me,
someone who is ***Three Times a Lady***,
in persona, interests, and accomplishments.
I had met ***A Natural Woman***.
I soon found that
We Belong Together,
and that I love you.
Just the Way You Are.

For the last decade,
you have been
Always on My Mind,

and **I Can't Stop Loving You**
So, I beg of you:
Stand by Me,
and *Love Me Tender*.
Remember that
This Guy's in Love with You,
and that
You Are the Sunshine of My Life,

Finally,
This I Promise:
You can always
Lean on Me and
Let's Stay Together.
Allow me to remain
Close to You.

You Make Loving Fun!

Haiku

Most successful men
Earn more than their wives can spend.
Smart women wed them

There are two key times
When men don't fathom women
Pre and post marriage

A true bachelor:
A man who has never made
The same mistake once.

For Kathy on Her 61st Birthday

I trust that retirement is as rewarding
as you hoped it would be.
I remember how I felt
in the months immediately following
my retirement in 1982.
I sensed relief from the heavy burden
of responsibility for the well being
and productivity of scores of people,
young and old, male and female,
military and civilian, enlisted and officer.
I also recall experiencing renewed energy
while expanding my professional interests
beyond writing journal articles and books.
I began to travel to
Canada, Indonesia, and Switzerland,
as well as across the United States.
After a few years of consulting travel,
I realized that I was essentially continuing my
practice of being away from my wife,
children, grandchildren, siblings, and friends
for days, weeks, even months, at a time.
I was again a vagabond and a truant.
So, I give up the charade
and tried to make up for the time lost
to my family and friends due to wartime
and federal service commitments and absences.
Unfortunately, the love of my life died
before I could make up for the lost years.
I regret that.
It is apparent that you have chosen a better path,
routine, and itinerary for your retirement
than the one chosen by your dad.

You have given your husband,
your children, your granddaughter,
your siblings, and your dad something special —
your time, interest, concern, and,
most important of all, your love.
I have also been privileged to see you
communicate, interact, and interrelate
with Tamra, Sean, your brothers and sister,
nieces and nephews, and most important,
your granddaughter, Kaila.
She is special in every conceivable way —
beautiful, engaging, bright, and loving —
obviously well worth the time, energy, and skill
you are investing in nurturing, guiding, training,
cherishing, and loving her,
one of my three great grandchildren.
HAPPY BIRTHDAY!

Haiku

Remember this truth:
Haste always results in waste
And ensures defeat

The sweetest revenge
Is to forgive the doer
With a heartfelt smile

Happy hour habit
A very dry Martini
Nectar of the gods

For Kaylyn on Her 13th Birthday

Today you become a teenager!
It is a very important phase of your life —
because it marks the beginning of adolescence,
the first phase of becoming a woman.
What can I tell you about that? Not much!
That conversation is better left to you and your mother.
Nonetheless, the teen years are a time for reflection —
a time to review the past, enjoy the present,
and plan for the future.
Here are my heartfelt wishes and prayers
for 2013 and your 13th birthday:
Good health, top school grades, loyal friends,
lots of love, and true happiness.
For those birthday wishes that are genuinely meant,
you should have the best and greatest year
that you've ever spent!
Worthy of your contemplation and reflection.
they are found in Frank Sinatra's song, *My Way*.
I have adapted a few stanzas just for you,
for they may highlight things that may be true
Read them carefully, and think deeply
about how they may apply to you.
Here are some Irish words of encouragement:
The Shamrock grows across the Emerald Isle,
good fortune in its wake.
When you believe all things can be,
success is yours to make.
May the Irish hills caress you.
May her lakes and rivers bless you.
May the luck of the Irish enfold you.
May the blessings of Saint Patrick behold you.

For Lina on Her Birthday

Another year has quickly vanished
for you as well as for me.
However, there is a very important difference
between the early forties and nineties.
Planning for the future is an exercise in futility for me.
Planning for the years ahead is indispensable for you!

I hope your birthday dreams and wishes
Will combine with all the rest
To fill your special day with happiness
And make it truly the best.

May your days be filled with joy
From morning 'till night
Each and every day filled with sunshine
And things for you to take delight!

May God bless you in the morning
With His presence shining bright
To make your whole day happy
With His radiant love and light.

May God bless you in the evening
When the daytime hours depart.
And like a blessing or special benediction,
Leave His peace within your heart.

HAPPY BIRTHDAY!

For Grace on Her 6th Birthday

This poem uses the ***Words of Love***,
the actual titles of love songs.
Those titles appear in bold italics
in the verses that follow.

Then Came You, the middle child
of my three great grandchildren.
The First Time Ever I Saw Your Face,
It was a photograph of a lovely ***Little Girl***.
In their letters and phone conversations with me,
your Nanna lauded your bubbling personality,
and your grandfather extolled
your awesome talents and your loving nature.

I have rarely been ***On the Street Where You Live***.
but you have been ***Always on My Mind.***
I am delighted, charmed, and enchanted
to have you as a loving great granddaughter.
You Light Up My Life!

Although I have not had a chance
to speak with you directly,
Have I Told You Lately?
that "***You Are My Sunshine***"
and **that** ***I Will Always Love You.***
Just the Way You Are?
Your Great Poppi will not be here to attend your wedding.
But remember this: ***I'll Be There*** in spirit.
And as long as God allows me to be here.
I'll stay ***Close to You***. All you have to do is
Reach Out & I'll Be There.
P.S. I Love You, Your Great Poppi

For Sean L. on His 35th Birthday

According to wise and watchful insurance actuaries.
you're almost half way between the years of your life span.
But they could be, and probably are, wrong.
Look at me, your grandfather, as exhibit A.
I never expected to live to be 90
and I am the only identifiable nonagenarian
in all of the recorded generations of the O'Neill clan!
And in addition, with the lengthening life span
of recent generations of American men
your age group could produce many centenarians.
That has happened at least once before on my mother's side
with one of your French Canadian Burgoyne ancestors.
Pierre Bourgoin, was born in Quebec, Canada
in 1641 and lived to be over 100!
Who knows? There could also have been
several Letellier centenarians
in earlier generations of your parents' families.
Anyway, I wish for you a long, healthy,
happy, productive, and rewarding life
with your lovely and loving wife, Leah.
I am pleased and proud of your accomplishments
as a successful entrepreneur and creative landscaper —
as well as an excellent judge of feminine beauty
and reliable spousal demeanor and prospects.
Here's a birthday wish as big as all outdoors:
Hoping and praying that the best things in life
will always be yours.
These wishes, from your Nanni and Poppi,
are just for you, our special grandson:
Simply everything that is joyful and rewarding
today and all the year 2013 through.
HAPPY BIRTHDAY!

For Leah on Her Birthday

Birthdays remind us of the passage of time
and the days and months that pass by faster
with every fleeting birth anniversary.
However, there are events of consequence
that occur every year
and are well worth remembering and assessing.
Although I have no idea what those incidents were
or why they loom large in importance,
you, and possibly only you,
can see and understand their significance.
Nonetheless they are your memories,
and that fact alone, make them noteworthy,
even historic or portentous.
So, you should take the time to review
the year just past to identify,
analyze, and evaluate those happenings to understand
their meaning and implications for the new year.
Believe me, it will be worth your investment
of the time and effort
you put into that demanding exercise.
Enough philosophy from your nonagenarian
grandfather-in-law!
My wishes and prayers for my lovely and loving
granddaughter-in-law:
Good health, interesting and achievable work challenges,
unconditional and unremitting understanding,
affection, support, and love
from your husband, Sean, your parents, siblings,
parents-in-law, your extended families, friends,
acquaintances, and coworkers —
and, above all, happiness!

For My 3rd Grandson on His 24th Birthday

I have heard nothing from you
in more than two years
no notes, letters, phone calls, or emails.
In short, you have not acknowledged
receipt of birthday and Christmas gifts
or your annual birthday verses
despite my repeated admonitions
and threats of their discontinuance.
It is not clear to me why you have abandoned
any interest in or concern about
the welfare of your paternal grandfather.
I am upset, troubled, and distraught about that.
I question what I have done or failed to do
to warrant your rejection.
I have not missed sending you presents
on your birthdays and Christmases
in the past 23 years
and for the last 15 years, I have added
an original personalized verse on your birthdays.
I believe that, at the very least,
you owe me an explanation —
preferably by return USPS mail
or a phone call to me any day or evening
at 508-394-9509.
Regardless, of your action or inaction,
you will always remain in my daily prayers
as you have been every single day of your 24 years.
I have not and will not desert or give up on you.
Although the gifts and verses
will not reappear unless and until I hear from you.
*****

And I just did!
I received your note and accept your apology.
So, the last few years of "no contact" are forgotten.
I leave the first part of this verse as a reminder
to my descendents of their obligation
to acknowledge all gifts promptly!
HAPPY BITHDAY!

Haiku

The only thing worse
Than a severe thunderstorm
a bad workday

A well-read person
Is a welcome visitor
Any day or time

It is easier
To forgive an enemy
Than to get even

Keep an open mind
Choose action selectively
The problem is solved

For Tamra on Her Birthday

Another 365 days have evaporated.
The years seem to fly by faster as we age,
and I certainly fit that category —
having reached the ripe old age of 90,
a birthday that I never believed I would reach!
The birthday party arranged by my family
was a complete surprise and a very gratifying one.
It was one of the two such parties I can remember,
The other was my 80th held in Rome, NY
when Kevin flew Else-Marie and me there and back.
I don't remember having a special party
or gifts when I was a child because my birthday fell
between Christmas and New Year's Day
in the era when children's birthdays
received very little attention and few lavish parties.
Your daughter Kaila is a very special child.
Not only is she loving, bright, and beautiful,
but she is also very talented.
Among the God-given gifts she displayed
in her captivating performance
were her sweet and on-pitch voice,
creative lyric-producing genius,
commanding presence, and outgoing persona.
Those are endearing traits and abilities,
but, when coupled with her independent and headstrong will,
they also promise some difficult times in her teen years.
However, success in controlling her
unyielding will and exuberance
will be well worth the extra effort.
You are a great mom and can handle it!
Happy Birthday!

For Bill Jr. on His 66th Birthday

In the verse that follows,
I have tried to find the perfect words
to tell you how much you're loved —
to let my eldest son know
how grateful for and proud I am of him,
despite the challenges and setbacks
that he has faced over the years —
and (hopefully) I trust, overcome.
It has always been difficult for me to describe
the feelings that I have deep inside
because life-changing and testing experiences
early in my life caused me
to conceal my thoughts and feelings.
Although I have often tried to find the perfect words
to say how much you're loved.
I have often been unable to voice them.
So, I have often failed to tell you
how much it means to me to have a son like you —
to tell you about the joy that comes from being loved,
and the confidence that accrues to being respected
and believed in by my son.
It is difficult for me to describe how much you mean to me
because you mean so much.
So, all that I can do now is tell you something
that I have not said to you often enough:
I LOVE YOU
and hope that those three words say it all.

For Sean T. on His 53rd Birthday

Another year has passed.
As we get older, they slip away quickly.
Your babies are now teenagers,
well on their way to adulthood
with all the opportunities and challenges
that status engenders.
As I have been privileged and gratified to observe,
Victor and Siara are not only
very bright and talented youngsters,
but also warm, highly personable, attractive,
mature, and loving adolescents.
Some of those qualities are inherited,
but the really important ones
are inculcated, developed, and nurtured
by parents, the paramount and ultimate teachers.
So, you and Lina have earned congratulations
and plaudits for fulfilling your responsibilities
and for outstanding performance
of essential parenting skills.
I'm sure that you fully understand the difficulties
and challenges of rearing children,
having observed your Mom and me
confronting the challenges, issues, and problems
posed by the lifelong job of rearing six children
all with different skills, talents, interests,
motivations, personalities, and goals.
Sometimes the tasks became overwhelming,
seemingly impossible to deal with
appropriately, adequately, and successfully.
Yet we persevered.
We never lost faith and did our very best.

On balance, I am happy with the results.
Although there were outcomes that were difficult
for the ones who experienced them,
we accepted them and tried to give them support.
We have a true family, consisting of sons and daughters
who have all experienced ups and downs.
Yet they remain positive and motivated.
Furthermore, our children truly love each other.
For that, I am gratified and grateful.
HAPPY BIRTHDAY!

Haiku

Buzz my feline friend
Obsessed with toilet water
Only when it's flushed

Sportsman's paradise
Boston's championship pro teams
Sox, Celts, Pats, Bruins

Rubber to home plate
Just sixty feet six inches
Baseball's key metric

An analog man
In today's digital world
A bad place to be

Blessed Pope John Paul
Recently beatified
Fast-tracked to sainthood

My Mothers

Please note the plural noun in the title.
It is not a typo — because I was blessed
with two loving and exceptional mothers.
One was my birth mother,
Pauline Eva (Burgoyne) O'Neill.
The other was her sister, my aunt,
Josephine Mary (Burgoyne) Tracey,
who later became my foster mother.

Pauline loved me so much
that, as she lay dying of acute peritonitis,
an infection from an appendix
that burst during my sister Eileen's birth,
she asked her older sister to take me
and my newborn baby sister, Eileen Ann,
home to Leominster with her
and rear us as our mother
for the remainder of our lives.

Josephine, childless for the four years
following her wedding to Eddie Tracey,
tearfully accepted that goodbye gift.
And my mother died that day
with the faith that she had made
a perfect choice and decision
for her sister and two youngest babies.

Josephine loved Eileen and me
with all her heart and soul
and carefully reared us to develop
into the caring adults we became.

Josephine was a remarkable woman.
Although she only attended school
as far as the third grade — leaving school only
to work on my grandfather's dairy farm
along with her 13 brothers and sisters.

Josephine also bore the burden
of a severe and cruel disfigurement — a port-wine
birthmark covering most of the left side of her face.
Her engaging personality and cheerful spirit
caused people to forget the defacement.
She was loved by many people of all ages.

She was also self-educated,
reading books and magazines voraciously,
speaking both English and French
fluently and grammatically—
and handling mathematics skillfully.
Her closest friend and frequent companion
was the principal of an elementary school.
So, I was truly blessed to have Josephine
as my mother for the remaining years
of her short life.

She died of a massive stroke at age 54.
I was alone in the hospital room with her
when she died and cried with my heart broken.
She was truly my mentor, protector,
advocate, supporter, booster, and inspiration —
as well as my best friend and true mother.
I regret that I never told her how much I loved her
— but I'm equally certain she knew that.....

For Kaila on Her 7th Birthday

This poem uses the Words of Love,
the actual titles of love songs composed by songwriters.
Those titles appear in bold italics in the verses that follow.
You are the eldest
of my three great grandchildren.
For that status, (*Have I Told You Lately*?)
as well as for many other reasons,
including your beauty, personal traits,
and God-given talents.
You Are My Sunshine
and ***I Will Always Love You!***
Just the Way You Are.
At my 90th birthday party,
I was enthralled by your ability
to compose wonderful songs
and sing them like ***a Shining Star***.
On many other occasions,
I was privileged to watch you dance,
performing like a gifted ***Party Doll***.
Unfortunately, I shall not be able
to attend your wedding,
but ***I'll Be There!*** in spirit.
I am delighted, charmed, and enchanted
to have you as a loving great granddaughter.
You Light Up My Life!
As long as God allows me to be here.
I'll stay ***Close to You***.
All you have to do is
Reach Out & **I'll Be There**.
Love, Grand Poppi

Kaylyn's Way

At 14 years, my end is far from near
Up to now, I've lived a life that's full
I've danced on more than a few highways
And more than that,
    I did it Kaylyn's way.

Regrets, I don't have any
I tried to do what I had to do
I planned each step along the byway
And much more than that,
    I did it Kaylyn's way.

Though I'm 14 and free to do what I choose,
That wrongly implies that I can't lose.
But that can't be the endplay.
I must ensure that I do it Kaylyn's way.
For that's the right and the only way.

For what has a girl got?
If not herself, she has naught
To say the things she truly feels
And not the one who kicks up her heels
The record shows I didn't quit
But did it Kaylyn's way!

There's only one way that's right for me
And that's the way it's gotta be
Not Mom's, Dad's, not Kolby's way
Or even Poppi's way,
The one and only Kaylyn's way!

My Little Girls

My Kathy and Maura
resisted arising
as the sun came up.
Stretching, yawning,
and squirming
like week-old pups.
Choosing their go-to-school clothes
with uncommon care,
knowing that their classmates
will be critical of the quality
and appropriateness
of the outfits they wear.
Grumbling about the familiar
parental demand
that they eat all their breakfasts
was carefully planned.
They nibble at the oatmeal
and sip the orange juice,
making faces all the while.
But, as the day goes by,
my little girls laugh and play.
They show me that they are special
in so many different ways.
So although I may fret and complain
about some unimportant things,
I treasure the love
that my little girls bring.

An Updated Assessment of My Only Godson, William (Bill) Raymond Camiré:
Son of Honoré L, Camiré and Bernadette C. Gariepy
Born in Leominster MA /April 16, 1957

What few people know about William Raymond Camiré:
Demonstrates more than a nodding acquaintance
with Rodale's *The Synonym Finder*
and *Webster's New Collegiate Dictionary*
An authentic autodidactic – a self-taught person. a person
who has learned a subject without the benefit of a teacher
or formal education.
Earned a Master of Photography certificate
from the Rhode Island School of Design in 2007
and a certificate in Computer Repair
and Networking from the CWF of Mashpee, MA,
affiliated with Comp TIA and Microsoft in 2002.
Selected by the American Society of Media Photographers
as one of 30 award winners among 1,600 US professionals
in 2007 for his photo of Walden Pond.
Received a certificate in Marine Maintenance and Master
Mechanic through the Mercury Inboard and Outboard
(I&O) in 2001 and 2002.
An authentic Dowser, a person with proven ability
to sense the presence of water under the earth
and in buried water mains.
Master of the art of remediating creative blockages,
such as creative blocks experienced by writers, artists,
musicians, painters, and photographers
An avid "birder" involved in studying birds of all species
in the wild, studying for more than 20 years
bird behavior and migration.

Served as a General Class Ham Radio operator
since 1982 with call sign and license KA1PNN.
Studied yoga for two years with Korea's famed
instructors, Bo-In and Namye Lee.
A documented speed reader, who for the past five years,
has read an average of 300+ books per year —
excluding novels but focused on in-depth research books
on a variety of subjects.

Things that people know about William Raymond Camiré:
Bill is:
Loyal as a family's collie
Protective as a German shepherd
Vulnerable as a young child
Bruises as easily as kick in the ankle
Forgiving as a doting parent
Bright as a polished silver dollar
Voluble as a talkative parrot
Thoughtful as a contemplative monk
Caring as a new father
Talented as a gifted violinist
Dedicated as a daily jogger
Determined as a frequent Kayaker
Inquisitive as an investigative reporter
The owner of vocabulary
as extensive as a published poet
Independent as a Siamese cat
Erudite as a Scholastic philosopher.
Imaginative as a unique compositor
and photo essayist
Holder of the gift of perfect pitch.

Some Things to Remember Always

Until you've grown up,
You'll never realize
How wonderful your parents are,
How kind, how loving, how wise —
You'll simply take for granted
From day to passing day
Every sacrifice they make for you
In their own sweet loving way.
But soon you'll grow and finally learn
The way that all humans do,
How much their love and caring
Has really meant,
And how thoughtful they've been too.

On Being a Dad

Dads don't have it easy
Hey seldom know
How to relate to others,
Particularly their older daughters,
Because they grew up not understanding
How to show love.
That's what happened to your dad
When he lost his mother at an early age
And learned how to mask his feelings
To avoid being hurt again.

Friendship

Don't spar with your friend
It's better to be yielding
Than to be correct

For Someone Very Special

You are not only a beautiful person
but also a caring friend.
We first met many years ago
when you were in your late 20s,
wearing your tasteful and stylish dresses
and your signature Windsong perfume.
You have long been known
by your young sisters
and seniors in nursing homes
as a friend and companion to those
who badly need friendship, affection, and help.

Ever loquacious and typically animated,
you always said what you felt
and meant what you said.
You invariably exemplified that old but true maxim:
A friend in need is a friend indeed.
To sum it up, you are not only a fascinating
and exceptionally bright and knowledgeable woman,
you have always been, and always will remain, my friend.
It is difficult for me to describe
how much you mean to me
because you mean so much.
So, all that I can do now is tell you something
that I'm sure you have known for a very long time
I LOVE YOU
and hope that those three words say it all.
HAPPY BIRTHDAY!

The Right Time

The "right time" to revitalize, expand, and extend
the love of our youth should have occurred
about 10 years ago when we became widowed.
The time has passed when one of us is committed
and seriously obligated to another person
who has life-threatening health problems.

Friendship is quite a different matter.
Closeness and companionship do not flower,
or even survive, dishonesty or infidelity.
They demand unfailing honesty, and faithfulness
— and invariably require caring about
and caring for another.

Over many years, for me that has meant
caring for you, my first true love,
and caring about your well being,
your physical, mental, and emotional health.
Although we have not seen each other
face to face in more than 70 years,
we remember the magical months of 1940-1941
when we were an item, very much in love.
and dating each other exclusively.

So, although it is unlikely that we shall ever
again see each other face-to-face,
now is the right time to renew and restore
our friendship and affection —
and most important, to remain in touch
through phone calls, greeting cards, and verse.

So let us rejoice that we can remain friends —
without guilt and with heart-warming memories
of our young adult years — the era of our first love!
That was a wondrous time, one never to forget.

You, now the warm-hearted, faithful widow,
mother, and grandmother,
the object of my admiration and affection,
both of us friends for 74 years —
and now is the very best time to be friends.
We are now nonagenarians.

Haiku

My friend in high school
Disappeared during the War
And never retuned

The only good friend
Who wrote to me frequently
Never made contact

Besides my dear wife
Jerri was the only girl
Who wrote frequently

For Janet

This bit of free verse uses the actual titles of songs
that relate in some way to what is happening
to you right now.
Those titles appear in bold italics
in the verses that follow.
Dear Heart:
This missive comes ***Straight from the Heart***
to a long-time lady friend
with a ***Heart of Gold***
written by Bill with all of his ***Heart and Soul.***
I know that you have been through a difficult time.
So, ***just Reach Out, I'll Be There***.
Lean on Me because ***You've Got a Friend***
Who has been there and done that
— two pacemakers, one for eight years
and the other for the past three years.
At Last, you're ready to ***Set the World on Fire***
without any concern about your atrial fibrillation —
because you and your rehabbed heart
can now be ***Happy Together***.
Soon you won't even think about your pacemaker
and not even try to ***Listen to Your Heart***.
And you won't have to worry about
Time After Time visits to C-Lab for blood work
to measure your INR
so that the now unnecessary daily dose of Coumadin
(due to a very new medication)
can be adjusted to maintain the proper level of
blood clotting (coagulation time) to prevent stroke,
which is a ***Rock Around the Clock***
preoccupation and worry of mine.

So, at the next wedding we attend
Let's Dance together.
That'll Be the Day,
one that is sure to be "*Some Kind of Wonderful.*
I close with this prayer:
May your thoughts be as glad as the shamrocks.
May your heart be as light as a song.
May each day bring you bright happy hours,
That stay with you all life long.

Haiku

My friend for 50
Just reach out, and she'd be there
Every single time!

Janet is special
Faithful and caring
Always a true friend

I have a true friend
She is dependable
With a heart of gold

She and I miss Jim
And we both miss Kay —
Her husband, my wife!

For My Friend Today and Always

Here are some of the words that describe my friend,
She is one of the most unforgettable friends
I have been lucky enough to admire,
know, and love for many years.
She is as:
Smart as a Jeopardy champion
Compassionate as an ICU nurse
Inquisitive as an archaeologist
Quick as a cricket
Bright as a new button
Pretty as a Hollywood starlet
Erudite as a Rhodes scholar
Cute as a button
Busy as a worker bee
Curious as a puppy
Warm as the autumn night
Sweet as a sugarplum
Lovely as a calla lily
Winsome as a close friend
Charming as a newly engaged woman
Endearing as a forehead kiss
Captivating as twilight
Engaging as an Irish storyteller
Independent as a woman can be
Stubborn when she's right
Talkative as a magpie
Happy as a little girl
Feminine as a woman should be
Loving as only a good friend can be.
So my friend is all of the above—
and much more, too!

I have just run out of words
to describe all of her
beguiling attributes and persona.
So, she has to know and understand
why and how much she is admired and loved
by everyone, including me!
HAPPY BIRTHDAY!

A Blessing for a Long-time Friend

May the blessing
of the soft warm Florida rain
fall on your body
and contentment be with you—
everywhere and always.

May the sun fall upon your face
so that all the beauty of your spirit
may be there for all to see.
May those gifts shed their sweetness
in the air for all to enjoy.

May the rain wash you clean and pure,
and leave behind shimmering pools,
where the blue of heaven shines—
and sometimes a star
to brighten your spirit.

May you be peaceful and happy
in your new home —
and pleased to have the company.
of your relatives close by
when you need them.

For Kiana on Her 18th Birthday

Today marks an important milestone.
Although you remain technically
a teenager, an adolescent, and a minor.
you are now legally of age —
which means that you are now an adult woman.
Inevitably, that status imposes
new restrictions and responsibilities
on both you and your friends, including males.
I leave it to your Mom, Dad, or Oma
to be specific about those boundaries,
obligations, and expectations.
I strongly recommend that you ask one of them
to discuss this critically important subject with you
unless they have already done so.
Until very recent years, supplemented
by occasional photographs,
I have observed your growth, development, and maturation
You have blossomed
into a strikingly lovely young lady.
Your Oma has told me that you are considering
a career as a hair stylist or beautician,
following the path set by your Mom.
Whatever career you choose,
you can be successful if you follow these rules:
Know who you are and listen to your heart.
Make a full commitment to your career.
Live for today and tomorrow instead of yesterday.
Commit emotionally, not just orally.
Learn how to communicate well in terms of voice,
speech, facial expressions, posture, and bearing
Enjoy your blessings and your life.
HAPPY BIRTHDAY!

For Kiana on Her 17th Birthday

Born on a Sunday, when Bill Clinton was president
and Al Gore was vice president,
Yahoo was founded in Santa Clara, California —
and a gallon of gas cost $109,
a postage stamp was 32 cents,
and a loaf of bread sold for $2.02.
You share your birthday,
,January 29th, with some famous people:
Anton Chekhov, the great Russian short story writer,
Tom Selleck, star if the TV series, Magnum, P.I.
and Blue Bloods,
Thomas Paine, Revolutionary patriot and writer
nd Oprah Winfrey, TV personality and long-admired host.
But, of far greater importance to me,
you are the only granddaughter of my best friend
and, for the last ten years, my constant companion,
Else-Marie Bowe.
Topping that status,
you are a young woman with distinctive attributes:
a personality that makes you appealing,
a demeanor that makes you appreciated,
an appearance and visage
that make you strikingly comely,
and talents that make you unique
and sought after by your peers.
And, most important of all,
you are loved unconditionally
by your doting father, Clarence.
HAPPY BIRTHDAY!

For Clarence's 46th Birthday

Although Father's Day passed June 15ʹ 2014.
every day of every year gives us an opportunity
to honor one of the most important men in our lives —
our dad, father, papa, poppi,
or whatever our affectionate name for him may be.

Birthdays are equally appropriate times
for such celebrations
because they are great days for reflecting
on the importance of fathers
and how your own father helped you
become the person you are today.

Here are some truisms that I'm sure
that Stacey, Kiana, and Else-Marie
know, understand, and appreciate
about their husband, father, and son.

Although they may infrequently,
even never, give voice to these beliefs,
I hope that you know
that they, too, know those axioms.
those, platitudes, those maxims—
because they are important facets
of your being, your persona,
your identity, your character.

You're someone who brings happiness
to everyone you know.
The world becomes a better place
wherever you go.

You're like a ray of sunshine
that gives life a warmer touch,
and that it is the special reason
you're admired and loved
by so many and so very much.

So, you will always be special,
you will always be loved
for the kindhearted way that you live.
And you will always be wished
joyful days in return
for the warmhearted happiness
that you never fail to bring.

I close this verse with my wishes for you:
May you have warm words on a cold evening,
A full moon on a dark night,
And the road downhill all the way to your door.
May your home be bright with cheer,
May your cares all disappear.
May contentment come your way.
And may laughter fill your day
On this, your forty-sixth
HAPPY BIRTHDAY!

Haiku

The man in your life,
Your father, is your guardian.
The man who loves you

For Kiana

Congratulations!
on momentous occasions and accomplishments:
First, on your high school graduation,
a most significant event in the lives of young people
because it is an important achievement
in one's path to adulthood.
Second, admiration is also due to you
for enlisting in the United States Marine Corps —
a celebrated component of the U.S. Armed Forces —
and a storied element of the seafaring soldiers
that I had the honor of serving with afloat during WWII
amphibious invasions, units ashore in Hawaii,
where I served with women Marines
early in their wartime history,
and then providing intelligence training
for Marine Corps members
during the Cold War (1970s) at Fort Devens.
I hope that you will take full advantage
of the opportunities for physical and mental growth,
emotional maturity,
and marketable employment skills
while you serve your country
Finally, I rejoice with and for you
on the presence in your life
of your loving parents and grandmother,
your Mom, Wendy, your Dad, Clarence,
and your Oma, Else-Marie.
Your Dad not only provided support for you
from the day you were born to the present,
but was also a continuing presence in your life,
by sharing responsibility for your upbringing and support

vacations, and attendance at events of importance
to you in your life both educational and recreational.
I wish only the very best for you in your Marine Corps
enlistment and for the many years that lie ahead.

Steve's Brother David, His Best Friend Forever

Bill T. had three brothers, Jim, the oldest,
and Frank and Jack,
born to his Dad's second wife, Sarah.
When he was a teenager
Jim and Bill remained very close
and shared many good years
until Jim died in 2001.
This, Bill knows very well:
brothers care, and brothers hold dear,
although they sometimes disagree and argue.
Nevertheless, an older brother
is always a very special friend.
Forever he epitomizes and is eternally family.
Steve, when you and your brother
were children and even adults, you often smiled
simply because David was your brother.
And you often laughed because there was nothing
our brother could do about it —other than laugh with you.
So, your friend, Bill, asks this
of his lifelong patron and Guardian Angel,
Saint Jude Thaddeus.
Please protect and guide through eternity
David, the "go to" Mottley for all of his siblings,
and always with Stephen at his side.
Because brothers are always there,
with laughter, love, and care.

For RCT Kiana on Her Graduation

Blessed with six grown children,
I have never missed an important event in their lives —
births, baptisms, birthdays,
graduations, weddings, etc.
That is normal and unremarkable for most parents.
That is not to say we never had arguments
or important, even critical, differences.
But we never stopped fully communicating.
However, I have recently learned
that your Dad did not attend your high school graduation
and that he has not been invited to attend your graduation
from Marine Corps Recruit Training —
a very significant and momentous event in your young life
Although I do not know the reasons,
do not want to know, and am fully aware of the fact
that it is none of my business,
I am troubled by that knowledge.
Your Dad has met his parental responsibilities
completely and in every respect.
He has not only provided support for you
from the day you were born to the present,
but he has also been a continuing presence in your life
by sharing responsibility for your upbringing and support
during vacations, and by attending events of importance
to you in your life both educationally and recreationally.
So, I am compelled by my affection
for both you and your Dad,
to implore you to repair your relationship
regardless of the cause of your disagreement,
difference, misunderstanding, altercation, quarrel, or tiff.
I ask you to invite him and your mother to your graduation
I promise that you will never regret it.

For Lucille on Her 91st Birthday II

Here are some of the clichés
that are apt and proper
for my first true love, Lucille Dolores
Lucille is as:
Quick as a cat and as busy as a bee
Bright as a silver dollar and as pretty as a daisy
Cute as a mouse and as lovely as a lily
Curious as a puppy and as alluring as a pinup
Sexy as a stripper and as slender as a sapling
Shapely as a Playmate and as charming as a princess
Built like a Playmate and as sharp as a scalpel
Urbane as a grande dame and as stubborn s a mule
Captivating as dimples and as winsome as a child
Talkative as a magpie and as happy as a lark
Endearing as a forehead kiss
Intriguing as a French accent
Engaging as an Irish raconteur
Independent as a lioness
Feminine as a woman should be
Loving as only a mother can be.
So Lucille Dolores is all of the above—
and much more, too!
I have just run out of words
to describe all of her
beguiling attributes and persona.
So, she has to know and understand
why and how much she is admired and loved
by everyone, including me.
HAPPY BIRTHDAY

For Kiana, A Lady Marine

One of the most difficult and challenging
physically and mentally of the basic training programs
conducted by the other military services.
the Army, Navy, Air Force, and Coast Guard.
Marine Recruit training
transforms the willing into the able.
Upon graduation from Recruit Training (Boot Camp),
enlisted young men and women are changed
from purpose-driven individuals into Marines —
a designation that will be a proud title
they will carry for the rest of their lives.
There are no "former Marines" or "exMarines."

As everyone who has undergone
Marine Boot Camp training knows,
Marine Corps training is a challenge that no one
who has not undergone it can fully comprehend.
It is 12 long weeks of trial, pain, and trepidation —
and for those who complete it,
it's a decisive, and meaningful victory.
It is that memorable day when the label Recruit
is removed and replaced
by the Eagle, Globe, and Anchor
and one becomes a Marine, —
a title reserved only for the few.

During my long lifetime,
I have met and served with many Marines,
males and females of all grades

and military specialties during war and peace,
at sea and ashore, in WW II and since,
in military and civilian settings,
from private to sergeant major,
and 2nd lieutenant to major general.
Without exception, they were all brave people
and outstanding military leaders.

My brother-in-law, Thomas B. Doheny, Jr..
also my best friend and close confidant,
was a Marine Corps Combat Medic
(a Navy Pharmacist Mate 3rd Class)
assigned to a First Marine Division landing force
during the invasion of the Pacific island of Peleliu.
Tommy was killed in action (KIA) September 15, 1944.

Semper Fi (Fidelis) Always Faithful

Remember this:

Semper Fi, Do or Die
So, Gung-Ho to go and pay the price
Here's to Leathernecks, Devil Dogs, and Jarheads
And Paris Island, SC in August, 2013. Semper Fi.

With Credit to song writer and vocalist, Trace Adkins
and Good Luck and Best Wishes for you.

Haiku

Once named a Marine
Never is an exMarine
Always a Marine

For Lucille

Of both English and French origin,
Lucille means "little light."
Of Spanish origin, the name Dolores,
means "Mary of the Sorrow."

However, the day commemorating
and honoring the first bishop of Ireland
is a happy one, not a melancholy one.
It is also a day when everyone is Irish!
So let us rejoice in this day together
By using Irish blessings and proverbs.

For each petal on the shamrock
This brings a wish your way -
Good health, good luck,
and happiness
For today and every day.

Oh, the music in the air!
And the joy that's everywhere -
Surely, the azure vault of heaven
was a grand and triumphal arch.
And the earth below was gay
with its tender green that day,
For the whole world is Irish
on the Seventeenth o' March.

May luck be our companion
May friends stand by our side
May history remind us all
Of Ireland's faith and pride.

May God bless us with happiness
May love and faith abide.

Leprechauns, castles,
good luck and laughter.
Lullabies, dreams,
and love ever after.
Poems and songs,
with pipes and drums.
A thousand welcomes,
when anyone comes.

Lucky stars above you,
sunshine on your way,
Many friends to love you,
joy in work and play.
Laughter to outweigh each care,
in your heart a song.
And gladness waiting everywhere,
all your whole life long!

Let me conclude with this assertion:
You are someone who listens to me
and makes me laugh,
someone who makes my life better
on a regular, rather than on
a "sometimes" schedule.
Because of you
I know what real closeness means.
And that's about as happy
as anyone can get.

For Clarence on His 45th Birthday

At the prime and notable age of 45,
you can count your many blessings.
Among the most important
are your wife, Stacey, daughter, Kiana,
mom, Else-Marie, and your superlative health.
So, although your have only lived
about one-half of the number of years
with which I have been blessed to reach,
you remain in good health and physical shape,
your mental acuity remains robust,
and your relationships are top-notch.
So, if you continue with a well-balanced diet
and regular fitness/exercise routine,
you should easily exceed my record of longevity.
To achieve that goal,
as well as continue feeling alive and relevant,
I also highly recommend that you
surround yourself with young people
as often and as much as possible.
Your daughter can provide much of that contact
and contribute to the fulfillment of that need.
Of course, Kiana will always be a wellspring
of youthful perspectives and activities for you.
I trust that you and she will take full advantage
of that all-important resource.
Here is my aspiration for you and Stacey:
Like your camping penchant and pastime,
my wish is as big as all outdoors —
and that the best things in life will always be yours!

I close with this Irish blessing:
May your mornings bring joy,
And your evenings bring peace.
May your troubles grow few
And your blessings increase.

Friendship

Ours is a friendship that I deeply treasure.
So vital, in fact, that it can't be measured.
I look into your eyes and see goodness there.
Your sensitive heart is replete with care.
I watch over you as you look out for me.
That is my promise — it will always be.
So, when trouble comes to call,
I'll do my very best to prevent your fall.
I'll protect you at every turn,
Our loving friendship
remains my closest concern.

Thank You

Thank you for that moment in time
when you said you are a friend of mine.
Thank you for that precious start
for you then truly won my heart.
Thank you for the many things you do,
but I thank you most for just being you.

For Our Twins

There are TWO things in life
for which parents are never prepared—TWINS—
although one in every 50 Americans is a twin,
and one in three is an identical twin.
The Tracey family was blessed with a set—
which, in their early years,
elicited the usual dumb questions:
Are they identical?
Which one is older?
Which is the "good" one?
How do you tell them apart?
Do you plan to dress them alike?
And in later years
people displayed skepticism
about their twinship:
Why don't they look exactly alike?
Why do they act differently?
Why do they have dissimilar personalities?
The answers to those questions
require more time than we have.
Suffice it to say that they:
Have identical DNA
Developed a close bond that exists to this day
with daily contact at least by phone
from Washington State to New Hampshire
using their special language
understood by no one else.
And, of course,
they required two of everything
including diapers, bottles,
cribs, carriages, toys,
attention, hugging, and love.

Haiku

Human encroachment
Crowding out other species
Result: ravishment

Sometimes you don't know
What you're really looking for
Until you find it

It's a real bummer
Viewing a boring movie
Like watching dogs eat

I did naught illegal
Is not the same as saying
I did nothing wrong

Living on Cape Cod
There's no other place like it
Excepting Heaven

One who reads a lot
Is always interesting
As a visitor

Choose food carefully
Fresh, tasty, and nutritious
To live a long life

For Else-Marie III

I know how badly life has treated you in recent years
and how difficult and painful
your physical problems have been:
The breast cancer, the colon cancer, your chemo and
radiation therapies, your surgeries, your eye problems
your hip replacement, and your broken collar bone
You are such a sweet, good-hearted, loving,
and lovable woman.
You have been very understanding
And in recent weeks and months, you have been very helpf
cleaning, grocery shopping, making beds, doing washing at
laundry, helping me with cooking, dish washing,
putting dishes away — and on and on.
You have been invariably good to me — and for me!.
I pray every night, and have for about six years,
for a cure for your cancers,
successful control of your eye diseases,
possible successful corrective surgery.
and a long, rewarding, and happy life.
I love you very much
and thank you for making the last 14+ years
memorable and happy ones.
I wish that I could stay here with your for many more year
but I cannot.
I am rapidly deteriorating, and I regret that.

Haiku

Fight global warming
Replace, reduce, or adjust
To save energy

A Special Prayer

Dear Lord,
Please give me a few good friends
who will love me for whom and what I am.
Keep ever burning brightly
before my wandering, my vagabond eyes,
the compassionate lights of trust and hope.
And though I may never come within sight
of the place of my wishes and dreams,
teach me to be grateful for the life I have lived,
and for the golden memories
that are good, unforgettable, and sweet.
And may the evening's twilight and following night
find me kind, gentle, and still worthy
in Your acceptance and love..

For My Special Great Granddaughter

You have a special place in my heart —
one that belongs only to you,
my beautiful, bright, loving,
and first great granddaughter,
It is a special place saved
for the times we have known at Cape Cod,
a special place for events we have shared,
and a place for wishes and dreams, too.
But the warmest place within my heart
is a wish for good health and happiness for you.
So, not a single day goes by wherever I am
that I don't thank God
and remember how lucky I am
to have a loving great granddaughter like you.
HAPPY BIRTHDAY!

A Wish for a Friend

Here are my wishes for you on this special day:
good fortune at your door, and laughter, too;
new friendships to warm your heart,
and old friendships that never end,
everyday your whole life through.
Wishing you a day of extraordinary miracles,
a day full of things to delight in,
a day in which everything is perfect,
a day of knowing that you're someone special
to your Mom and Dad, your children,
your friends, and to your Poppi.

HAPPY BIRTHDAY!

Haiku

Nature gone wild:
Hurricanes, floods, tornadoes
Earthquakes and wildfires

WAR

Most were just young kids
Who had seen little of life
But were shown Hades

Leadership

Lead your organization, whether military or civilian.
Always and when necessary, use words.
Leaders are always on stage,
playing before a live, critical and crucial audience.
They must model the behaviors
they expect from their subordinates.
So, it is not so much something they do.
It's more a matter of whom they are.
They profoundly influence tomorrow's leaders
of their organization or unit for good or for bad.
That is a very weighty responsibility,
one that they must never shun or shirk.
Effective leaders are highly visible
They are often out and about
Frequently and regularly they are
away from their offices
and around the plant, building, range, or field,
seeing and being seen —
and keeping their finger
on the pulse of the organization,
not just attending interminable meetings,
formations, or drills,
but in face-to-face,
often one-on-one interactions
with their people.
That is genuine, real, and authentic leadership.
Practice it vigilantly and consistently.

Remembering War

Whether a sunny or a cloudy day
the sounds of flapping cotton
and clanking halyards ride the waves
of fresh salt air that rush past me.
But, I'm not on the bridge
of a warship in the South Pacific
as I was seventy years ago.
The flapping and clanking
are caused by the Cape Cod wind
whipping the Stars and Stripes
that fly daily on a twenty-foot flagpole
in my front yard — my pride and joy!
Every time I hear those familiar sounds,
my heart fills with emotion
remembering those long days and nights —
far away from home and family —
standing watch as officer of the deck
as we steamed toward the Philippines.

We were a part of a large armada
of warships of all types and sizes, battleships,
cruisers, destroyers, and landing craft,
on their way to the invasion of Leyte.
It was my first taste of combat action,
and I was nervous and apprehensive.
But we made the repeated landings
unscathed and successfully,
unloading tanks, trucks, troops, and supplies,
despite the Kamikazes, suicide swimmers,
mortar fire, artillery, and snipers.
We were the crew of the USS LST 117,
later dubbed the Lucky 11-7.

When the war ended several months later,
my luck held!
I came home to my wife and got on with my life—
pursuing fulfillment as a parent and teacher
with the deep sense of appreciation
unique to survivors of war.
However, many soldiers, sailors,
Marines, and Coasties did not survive.
I often think about them, the men and women,
including my 19-year-old brother-in-law,
who were killed in action in World War II —
and in other wars from the Revolutionary War
to the Korean War and Vietnam —
as well as the Gulf, Iraq, and Afghanistan.
And I remember with sadness
those who lived but came back mutilated, disabled,
PTSD, or haunted by their experiences to go home
and lead normal lives, as well as the thousands
of men and women in VA hospitals
for the rest of their lives.
We owe those soldiers, sailors, airmen, Marines,
Coasties, and nurses—
those who sacrificed so much to defend
our flag and our liberties—
our thanks, prayers, and support,
not just on Memorial Day
but also on every other day of the year.

My Academic Year
At the U.S. Army War College

Interviewed and nominated in March 1967
by a special DA Selection Board at the Pentagon
for admission to the 1968 Class of the USAWC.
That singular honor was offered to me
after completing ten years of service
at the USASATC&S, Fort Devens, MA,
sequentially as psychologist,
educational consultant, and director of instruction,
GS 13 and 14 and GM 15.

Reported to the USAWC August 9, 1967
and assigned quarters in a magnificent two story mansion
dismantled, moved from Germany, and reconstructed
in Carlisle, Pennsylvania.
It contained an imposing entrance and reception room,
a double staircase (one up and one down), six bedroom suite
a well-equipped large kitchen and separate pantry,
several function rooms, a den and library,
a large living room with an enormous stone
fireplace, a surrounding moat,
and underground "escape" tunnels.
Then called "The Castle,"
it now serves as the Commanding General's quarters.

The six fortunate occupants were two Army Colonels (O6
two lieutenant colonels (O5),
and two civilians — both GS 15s, one an ASA/DAC,
and the other a DIA civilian.
Numbering 205 students, all members were either
Army, Marine Corps, or Air Force

lieutenant colonels/colonels (O5s or O6s),
Navy commanders/captains (O5s or O6s),
or upper grade civilians (GS 15 or above),
representing the CIA, DA, DIA, DOS, NSA, or USIA.

The 10-month course provided
social and professional friendships,
as well as demanding intellectual challenges
and unique educational opportunities.
The social events included formal military balls,
"Dining In" formal dinners, individual and team sports,
and committee and small group dinner parties.
Each of the nine academic courses required
day and evening committee work and individual
intensive reading and study, library research,
and both written and oral reports — all graded.

Surprisingly, the writer (a civilian) was selected
to be the student responsible for chairing the committee
established to organize and manage the subcommittees.
Those groups were tasked to identify
the strategies needed to respond to the strategic
and tactical issues during the computer-assisted
two-week exercise.
The war game involved the entire class of 205 Army, Navy,
Air Force, and Marine Corps officers.
It was titled Course 6, Army and Theater Capabilities
in Selected World Areas.

The USAWC Class graduated on June 10,1968
Many grads later became Army, Marine Corps,
or Air Force generals — or Navy admirals —

and some were promoted to two, three,
or four stars before retiring from their branch of service.
In retrospect, it was a wonderful career changing
lifetime experience!

Haiku

The close friends you make
In a military school
Remain friends for life

Practical training
Is always a priceless gift
For all grunts and gobs

A career builder
U.S. Army War College
A respite from war

A real enigma
U.S. Army War College
Where peace is the goal

Twin Towers payback
Bin Laden's execution
A justified kill

Justice has been served
Osama bin Laden killed
Let us be thankful

We Play "War"– Often!

Beginning in grade school,
we played "King of the Hill" —
where the objective was to keep other players
from reaching the top of a hill
by physically pushing them back.
In later childhood,
the game was either "Cowboys and Indians"
(or just "Cowboys," where the weapons
were either cap guns
and/or homemade bows and arrows.
In adolescence, war games took
any one of several different forms: —
from street or neighborhood gangs,
or less formal rough games
similar to football or rugby,
without many, if any, rules.
About that time, games began to include
board and computer games
such as checkers and chess, to Risk, Tactics,
and Global Domination, Dungeons and Dragons, Contract
Bridge and various forms of Poker,
Axis and Allies, Illuminati to Diplomacy,
and Medieval, the Civil War, World Wars I and II,
and many wars fought since.
So war is a human activity
that has occurred throughout the ages
and is likely to continue
despite attempts to end all wars.

Off to the Pacific War

We kissed goodbye in the darkness
at the bottom of the gangway
of the troop ship berthed
at the San Francisco Embarcadero.

Soft were her lips
as I pressed them to mine.
Warm as her tender heart
and sweeter than wine.

Streaked were her soft cheeks,
wet with her tears.
Reflecting the warmness
of summer night sky and sea,
were the eyes of the woman
that God gave to me.

As I climbed up the brow,
I turned back to wave
at the vision of loveliness
that I was forced to leave.

The ship soon got underway
and, as we passed under the Golden Gate,
I felt cold, depressed, and downhearted,
wondering if I would ever return
to the love of my life.

Nature

A wonder to see
An osprey diving for fish
To attract his mate

Bird Breeding Season

June is the month to observe the rituals
of Cape Cod's resident birds.
It is the breeding season for
American robins, chickadees,
swallows, gray catbirds, and many other species,
including beach and sea birds,
such as terns, piping plovers, and oystercatchers.
So spring is the time when birds
are fully engaged in the nesting cycle.
The sequence begins with courtship
and progresses through nest building,
egg laying, covering the eggs,
rotating and incubating the eggs,
feeding the young, overseeing the fledging,
and, in some cases, re-nesting
after the first brood has fledged.
Technology applications permit the observation
of the nesting cycle without interfering with the process.
It requires the attachment of a tiny camera to the inside
of the nest or birdhouse and running a wire into a TV
inside the house, where stunning views
of the process can be observed at any time..
During the nesting cycle, the birds must also
protect their nests from predatory hawks, owls,
vultures, dogs, cats, and nest-robbing crows—
even curious humans— after being alerted
to the danger by the alarm calls of other birds.
In my case, as well as the situation of other
owners of birdhouses,

the nest building phase includes cleaning out the
remnants of the prior year's nest,
and replacing the straw, moss, twigs,
and other nest building materials
for the new brood.
A small investment of time looking
in a field guide and paying close attention
to the behaviors of your feathered
neighbors will reward you and also last a lifetime.

New England Lobster

Highly nutritious and a weight-watcher's dream, Lobster is
in fat, calories, and cholesterol, and lower in all of those diet
advantages than lean ground beef and skinless white chick
and turkey meat.
Lobster meat also registers high in amino acids, potassium a
magnesium, vitamins A, B12, B6, niacin and riboflavin,
calcium and phosphorus,
iron and zinc.
To achieve those healthful benefits, diners, whether at home
in a seafood restaurant, should not waste any eatable part o
lobster.
Observations over more than 80 years reveal that few peop
outside of New England know how
to eat a lobster, leave too much eatable and delicious lobst
meat on their plates — and that wind up
in the garbage can.

How to Eat Lobster

.ing lobster requires proper tools, hand and arm strength, and
considerable time and patience.
e tools include a nutcracker, a small three-pronged fork, and
a sharp pointed (pick-like) tool.
When the lobster has been cooked and cooled enough
to handle without gloves or mittens,
start by grasping the lobster with both hands and
twisting off the two claws.
Then crack each claw with the nutcracker and
remove the meat with the fork and/or pick,
and drop it into melted butter.
Eat these pieces while they are warm.
Next, separate the lobster tail from the body
by arching the back until it cracks and is detached.
en, bend the tail back, break the flippers off the tailpiece and
ick and insert the fork where the flippers broke off and push
the meat out the other end of the tail.
that fails, cut open the half-circle rib-like structures (or cut
them with a knife), spread the tail open,
and remove the tail meat in one piece.
Open the tail from top end to bottom to reveal the large
intestine —remove it in one piece and discard.
 it breaks or leaks, wash the tail in hot water to remove the
contents of the intestine.
Save the tail to reheat for one minute in boiling water
Dip in melted butter and eat.

Unhinge and remove the back (including the long "feelers" a
eyes), remove the "tomalley," the soft green substance,
and save that delicacy for the many or
few "confirmed" lobster eaters.
The red waxy substance, the roe or coral,
although edible, may be discarded,
although it can be finely chopped and used later
as an ingredient, along with other lobster bits and pieces, t
make lobster bisque.
Next, open the body and crack it sideways,
where small round pieces of lobster meat
can be found and removed with the pick.
Last of all, the small legs and claws
contain delicious meat.
Either suck the meat out or push it out
using the blunt end of the pick.
Eating a lobster is time-consuming
and requires both expertise and persistence.
The ritual, however, is worth the time and effort!

Haiku

Keep the oil flowing
The pump price low and stable
Result: lower costs

A business truism:
People must be monitored
To avoid mistakes

Gulls and Terns

There's a moment at dawn
When the clouds over the sea
grow plum and lavender
and the gulls and terns scatter,
winging above the water,
gliding gracefully onto the swells
bobbing and pitching
with the dancing waves.

The Sea

As I look out to sea
what I can of the sea,
It is a marvelous sight.
Light from above
shimmering on the waves,
touching my eyes,
a joyous sight
as I look out to sea
to see what I could see.

Haiku

Sometimes you don't know
What you're really looking for
Until you find it

Surviving Nemo

As I write this missive,
I watch the snowflakes flying
and the leafless trees bending,
both enduring the onslaught
of gale-force winds.
Although it is a cold and sunless day,
hopefully we shall not have to deal with
a reprise or encore of the wrath
and destruction of Nemo
during the period Friday, February 8
through Tuesday, February 12.

The first night of the storm
was horrendous —
a real test of ability to survive.
Without electrical power,
I had no lights, heat, or ability
to make or receive phone calls.
The Yarmouth police checked on my well-being —
and with my neighbor — to determine
whether I should be moved to a public shelter
or to a neighbor's home.

The move was made to my across-the-street friends
of many years, the Camiré domicile,
there, Bernadette, my friend for more than 60 years,
and her son, William Raymond Camiré
my only Godson, came to my rescue!
Bill repaired a gas-fired floor heater.
to provide needed warmth.

Bernie prepared and served hot food
to please and satisfy the palate and stomach,
and gave me sole possession of the couch
for three nights of much needed sleep.

By those actions, my hosts permitted me
"To let a smile be my umbrella"
for several cold and trying days,
and allowed me
"To Direct My Aging Feet"
to *"The Sunny Side of Evergreen Street,"*
which only shows that
when a friend is down
and dangerously near out,
the Camirés lifted their voices
to enthusiastically shout,
"Come on Over" to weather the storm out.

Let me close with these song titles,
which clearly convey
the underlying themes of this verse:
"Leaning on You"
"I'll Be There for You"
"We're All In This Together"
"That's What Friends Are For"
"Thank You for Being My Friends"
and
"Standing by Me."
Love,
Bill
2/17/2013

The Blizzard of 2013 on Cape Cod

On Friday morning, the eighth of February,
a massive Nor'easter hammered the Cape
with howling winds and blinding snow.
It was named "Nemo" by The Weather Channel.
Newspapers also called it "Wintercane."

Cape Codders hunkered down
as hurricane-warning flags snapped
in the wind at Coast Guard stations.
By 7:30 p.m., gusts reached more than 50 mph,
and power outages plagued the place made for vacations.

Downed trees and wires were the cause of the outages.
Before it was over, winds achieved
hurricane strength of 84+ miles per hour.
And as many as 130,000
NStar customers were without power.

In Yarmouth, 97 percent of customers
were without electricity, some for four or more days.
Even the iconic Nauset Light went dark.
Snow accumulation varied from 8 to 17 inches.
So, for Cape Codders, Nemo was no "walk in the park."

Without electricity, heat, or lights,
candles and board games replaced
television, books, and newspapers for diversion.
Even the kids, with schools closed and windy conditions,
were deprived of snow-centered recreation.

The brave souls who chose to weather the storm,
rather than seek refuge in one of the town shelters,
hunkered down with layers of clothes in their 40-degree
darkened homes without a heater to warm their toes.

Others, some with their pets, were transported
by police, firefighters, and volunteers,
to shelters in Falmouth, Yarmouth, and Sandwich,
where cots to sleep on, hot meals to comfort them,
and fellowship enabled hem to endure the long watch.

Those who failed to fill their cupboards
and put gas in their cars were forlorn.
To keep vehicles out of the way of snowplowing trucks,
Governor Patrick issued an executive order
banning vehicle travel and leaving many people stuck.

Travel by other means was nearly impossible.
Bus service of the Cape Cod Regional Transit Authority
and steamship authorities at Woods Hole,
Martha's Vineyard, and Nantucket suspended service.
So for three or four days no one could even take a stroll.

People near the shore, especially in Sandwich,
had front row seats for the rising storm surge.
Flooding, erosion, unstable bluffs, dune destruction,
and damaged or destroyed homes,
were the price tags for the storm's devastation.

The big question is apparent; is global warming to blame
for the hurricanes, tornadoes, floods, droughts,
and blizzards of recent years?
Regardless, Nemo taught us one important lesson:
is past time to bury Cape Cod's power lines under ground.

Trials and Tribulations

We had a lot of trials in our time,
Such as when we didn't have an extra dime.
And skimping on the food we had to eat,
we even had to ration the heat.
And the grocery and milk bills
piled up without end,
Leaving us with little or nothing to spend.
But somehow we managed to make it through.
Six kids and a house, even a car or two.
Although we didn't have much money on hand,
we stuck together as
The Tracey band.

Giving and Forgiving

What makes life worth living
Is our giving and forgiving,
And leaving tiny bits of kindness
That will leave joy behind us.
And forgiving bitter trifles
That the right words often stifles —
for the little things are bigger
than we often stop to figure.
What makes life worth living
Is outgiving and forgiving.

Miscellany

Odds and ends engage
And mesmerize the reader
Read on to find out

On Reaching the Age of 90

As one gets closer to the end of life,
and despite attempts to ignore that reality,
they invariably come to the fore of consciousness.
At times they produce fear and dread.
At other times they engender hope
and trust in the possibility of going to
Heaven to be with God,
his Blessed Mother, the Angels and Saints,
and the members of our family and friends
who have gone before us in the State of Grace.
People of most faiths believe that,
if they have obeyed the rules of life,
as established by God,
they can enjoy eternity in His presence.
Yet, it is difficult to believe that we have lived
the kind of life that will warrant, even guarantee,
that we will be eligible to enter Heaven —
or even Purgatory — following our death.
Every human being has imperfections,
which have resulted in transgressions
and violations of the laws of God.
Roman Catholics believe they can be absolved
of sin, even very serious transgressions,
if they die in the State of Grace,
having shown true sorrow for those sins,
and confessed them to a priest
in the sacrament of Penance.
Yet, there are likely to be doubts
that we have invariably
confessed all of our sins
and were always sorry that we had disobeyed
the laws of our Maker.

So that uncertainty or misgivings about them
come into our consciousness all too often
— resulting in concerns about
our final destination, Heaven, Purgatory, or Hell,
following our death.
All that we can do to ensure
that we achieve our ultimate goal of salvation
is to make the best confession
that we can make as often
as we can, at least monthly,
for the remaining years of our life.
That is my intention,
the action that I have been taking for the past two year
and will continue to honor,
from now to the end of my life.
I hope and pray that will become
the goal and practice of all my children, grandchildren
great grandchildren, their spouses and later descendant
of the Tracey-O'Neill family.
May God Bless every one of You!

Haiku

Blessed Pope John Paul
Recently beatified
Fast-tracked to sainthood

As a boy I did
What my father demanded
When is it my turn?

Boiled New England Lobster

Whether it is baked stuffed, boiled, or steamed,
Lobster is one of my favorite meals
and a delicious dinner for one, two or a dozen.
More plentiful and cheaper in the summer,
choose chicken lobsters (1 to 2 1/2 pounds,
select (2 ½ to 3 pounds, or jumbos
(3 and up to 14 pounds) — or culls,
which have only one claw
and are somewhat less expensive per pound.
When selecting lobsters,
look for the most active ones,
those whose tails curl under the body
and hang down, when the lobster is picked up.
I prefer to boil lobsters because it is faster,
easier to control cooking time,
and less difficult to remove the meat from the shell.
Use a pot size large enough to hold the lobsters.
Fill the pot to ¾ full with clean Atlantic ocean water —
or tap water containing 1/3 cup of salt per gallon.
Use more than one pot if needed.
Plunge lobsters head first into the boiling (rolling) water,
and allow the water (uncovered) to return to slow boil.
Cook (weight of individual lobsters) chicken, 8 minutes,
2 lbs, 15 minutes, 2 1/2 lbs, 20 minutes, 4 lbs, 32 min,
and 6 lbs, 48 minutes
Serve immediately, if removed from pot and cooled,
reheat in boiling water one minute
then serve with hot melted butter.
Bon appetite!

A Tutorial on Lyme Disease

Lyme Disease, the Northeast's challenging health threat,
is spread by the black-legged deer tick.
These insects are carried by deer and dropped off
into long grass where they crawl or fall
onto their human hosts.
When ticks bite, they also inject bacteria,
which cause the disease —
or one of several other tick-related illnesses.
Protection against tick bites is provided
by clothing, best when treated with Permethrin
(available in many sporting goods stores)
48 hours in advance of possible exposure.
Potential victims should perform frequent tick tests,
shower or bath daily, using DEET
or other insect repellants on their skin
while outside, and wear tick repellant.
They must also keep their arms and legs or other body par
completely covered with clothing and insect spray.
It wise to wear long pants
and tuck them into their socks
before venturing into long grass or woods.
Symptoms of the disease include a circular rash
around the site of the tick bite,
and neurological and facial muscular problems.
Other symptoms may include fatigue and muscle aches,
fever, drenching sweats, shaking chills,
severe headaches, shortness of breath, lightheadedness,
unsteadiness of the body, and chest pain.
Since 2006 more than 8,000 ticks have been sent
to the UMass Laboratory of Medical Zoology
to be tested for the disease.

That program was funded by a state grant to test 100 ticks
from 32 Massachusetts towns, including Nantucket
and all 15 Cape Cod towns.
Testing is available through offices at all Cape Cod towns
and Nantucket island.
Additional related problems, include other testing labs
and Lyme-literate physicians.
Most insurers do not cover tests
that are not recommended by the Federal government.
Alternative tests cost between $100
and more than $1,000.
New cases of Lyme disease number about 300,000
every year in the United States
and more than 75 percent of them are
in the Northeast.
Barnstable County on Cape Cod has the highest number
of cases in the US.
New cases number about 300,000 every year
in the United States.

Haiku

Lyme disease is dire
Deer ticks are the carriers
Contract it and weep.

Prevent Lyme disease
It demands life-long treatment
To control symptoms

Chevrolet Malibu Recalls

I bought a new Chevrolet Malibu in October 2004
and maintained it for the ensuing 10 years in accordance wi
the maintenance schedule contained in the Driver's Manua
Besides minor repairs, the only major
maintenance job was the installation of
a complete set of replacement brakes
and brake parts in 2012,
at a cost of $1,001.00.
The dealer's maintenance team recently informed me that n
car requires a complete replacement of the exhaust system
from the manifold back to the tailpipe – at an estimated cost
$800.00.
Recently, I received three safety recall notices from the
Chevrolet company as detailed below:

All three notices apply to my 2004 model year Chevrolet
Malibu VIN 1G1ZS52F54F150553

June 2014, Recall 14116: GM is recalling the steering colur
replaced under Customer Satisfaction Program 004050. GM
recalling the torque the torque sensor assembly on the under
of the steering column that was installed in the vehicle.
The vehicle, equipped with EPS, may experience a sudden l
of power steering assist that could occur at any time whil
driving, which could result in increased risk of a crash.

June 2014, Recall 14152: The vehicle has a condition in wl
the transmission cable may fracture at any time, which ma
cause the driver to be unable to select a different gear, rem
the key from the ignition, or place the vehicle in
park, thereby increasing the risk of a crash.

all three cases, the notice states that parts to repair the defect are not currently available and that when parts become available, the repairs will be serviced without charge —and that a letter requesting that the vehicle be taken to a Chevrolet dealer for servicing will be sent when parts are available.

July 2014, Recall 13036: Increased resistance in the Body Control Module (BCM) connection system, resulting in voltage fluctuation in the Brake Apply Sensor (BAS) circuit that can cause service brake lamp malfunction. These conditions may increase the risk of a crash.

Meanwhile, the risks of crashes remain, unless a replacement vehicle is made available without charge.
No such offer has yet been made.

Haiku

What is not checked
Often gets out of control
Let that be your guide

It is easier
To forgive an enemy
Than to get even

A generous man
Who refreshes others in need
Will himself be helped

Cape Cod's Fields of Dream

Founded in 1885,
the Cape Cod Baseball League (CCBL)
is a summer baseball alliance of ten teams
on Cape Cod in Massachusetts.
The league now includes teams that play a
44-game regular-season schedule
and a postseason made up of
best-of-three quarterfinal, semifinal,
and championship series.

Many Major League Baseball players
started their careers in college.
During the 2014 MLB season, 30 CCBL
Alumni made their major league debuts.
The list included 20 pitchers
and 10 position players.
As of July 2014, the number of all-time
CCBL alumni in MLB totaled 1,056,
more than any other
summer collegiate league.
The CCBL Hall of Fame is located
in the "Dugout," the lower-level
of the JFK Hyannis Museum.

In alphabetical order,
the CCBL team names and the location
of their home fields are as follows:

Bourne Braves,
Doran Park, Upper Cape Regional Tech, Bourne
Brewster Whiteeaps
Stony Brooke Elementary School, Brewster
Chatham Anglers
Veterans Field, Chatham Center,
Cotuit Kettleers
Lowell Park, Lowell Ave. Cotuit
Falmouth Commodores
Guy Fuller Field, Falmouth
Harwich Mariners
Whitehouse Field Harwich High School
Hyannis Harbor Hawks
McKeon Park, downtown Hyannis
Orleans Firebirds
Eldridge Park Orleans
Wareham Gatemen
Clem Spillane Field, Wareham High School
Yarmouth-Dennis Red Sox
Red Wilson Field, Dennsis-Yarmouth Regional High

For many professional baseball players
CCBL's teams have unquestionably
provided their "fields of dreams,"

Some Well-known CCB Hall of Famers

Scott Atchison, Boston Red Sox
Mile Aviles, Cleveland Indians
Jackie Bradley, Jr. Boston Red Sox
Daniel Bard, Texas Rangers
Jacoby Ellsbury, New York Yankees
Evan Longoria, Tampa Bay Rays

Justin Masterson, Cleveland Indians
Scott Sizemore, New York Yankees
Mark Teixeira, New York Yankees
Chase Utley, Philadelphia Phillies
Kevin Youkilis, Boston Red Sox

Some CCBL/MLB Coaches

John Farrell—Toronto Blue Jays/Boston Red Sox
Joe Girardi— Florida Marlins/New York Yankees
Bobby Valentine—Texas Ranger/NewYork Mets/Boston R
Sox

Other CCBL/MLB Players

Carlton Fiske—Boston Red Sox
Nomar Garciapara—Boston Red Sox
Mike Glavine—New York Mets
Mike Lowell—Boston Red Sox
Kevin Millar—Boston Red Sox
David Ross—Boston Red Sox
Nick Swisher—New York Yankees
Mark Teixeira—New York Yankees
Chase Utley—Philadelphia Phillies
Jason Varitek—Boston Red Sox
Brandon Workman—Boston Red Sox

Haiku

The hitter's best dream
Single, double, triple, homer
Hit for the cycle

Attaining Sobriety and Other Human Frailties

Why do people become alcoholics?
Addicted to tobacco?
Surrender to habitual sin?
Are they due to weaknesses? Vulnerabilities?
Character flaws? Iniquity? Carnality?
Depravity? Susceptibility? Self indulgence?
Predispositions? Lack of mental discipline?
Defects? Mental illness??
Shortcomings? Ignorance?

Or are they due to imperfections?
Tastes? Penchants? Desires?
hat is the solution— the means of quitting once and for all?
If a person truly wants to stop those consuming
and life-shortening habits,
answer lies in commitment to a decision, once and for all,
to quit the habit or behavior,
to avoid the persons, places, or conditions
that give rise to the habits to reject, renounce,
and to forswear, ditch, reject, and disown
all of the foregoing,

Haiku

Be happy today
Tomorrow may be harder
Make the adjustment

You made me love you
I didn't want to do it
But I did love you

About Me

A walking collection of inconsistencies
and contradictions
A person with both good and bad habits
A nonagenarian, a very old man (90s)
A World War II Navy amphibious combat veteran
A motherless baby at 16 months.
An adopted child at age 16
A college graduate with advanced degrees
A former teacher and college professor
A retired DA civilian, GM 15
A husband for 53 years and a widower for 17
An international HR consultant
An avid reader of books, newspapers, and magazines.
A part-time philosopher
A published writer of 14 professional books
100+ articles, and 5 anthologies of poetry
A lifelong physically active person
in team and individual sports (basketball,
soccer, gymnastics, cheerleading, golf,
swimming, and bicycling).
A Red Sox, Patriots, Celtics, and Bruins fan
A TV sports fanatic.
An authentic and conscientious leader
A reluctant but faithful follower.
Once a heavy drinker, now a teetotaler.
A long-time Democrat who regularly voted Republican.
Now an unenrolled liberal-conservative.
A loving parent of six, grandparent of 12,
great grandfather of three, and Godfather of three
Often a loner. Always a lover.
That's me in my mirror!

A Final Message

The people and events described in this volume of
Strands of Memory are important and significant
in the story of my life.
I love or loved every one, whether named or
unidentified, in its verses.
They meant everything to me.
So I close with
a heartfelt thank you to my family and friends
for their love — and a final prayer of gratitude
for their part in my long life.

Sincerely,
Bill Tracey

Index

If you can't be good
Always be dependable
And you'll be valued